DR KAY KUZMA
A HUG & A KISS
AND A KICK IN THE PANTS

LIFEJOURNEY
BOOKS

DAVID C. COOK PUBLISHING CO.
ELGIN, ILLINOIS • WESTON, ONTARIO

LifeJourney Books is an imprint of David C. Cook Publishing Co.

David C. Cook Publishing Co., Elgin, Illinois 60120
David C. Cook Publishing Co., Weston, Ontario

A HUG AND A KISS AND A KICK IN THE PANTS
© 1987 by Kay Kuzma

Cover by Edward Letwenko

First Printing, 1987
Printed in the United States of America
92 91 90 89 88   5 4 3

Kuzma, Kay.
    A hug and a kiss and a kick in the pants/Kay Kuzma.
        p. cm.
    Includes index.
    ISBN 1-55513-339-8
    1. Family—Religious life. 2. Discipline of children—Religious aspects—Christianity. I. Title.
BV4526.2.K89 1987
248.8'4—dc19

                                                              87-20318
                                                                  CIP

DEDICATION

To my son, Kevin, who inspired this book and unselfishly gave me permission to use personal illustrations so other families could discover the joy of creative discipline.

And to the other precious Kevins of the world, that through the love and understanding of you, the reader, they may learn to know their loving Father in Heaven and be led to willingly respond to His call, "Come unto Me."

ACKNOWLEDGMENTS

Each story in this book is a treasure given to me by moms and dads, grandparents, aunts and uncles, and friends who have experienced the joy of "training children in the way they should go." Thank you each one—wherever you may be. Sometimes I used your real names. I hope you don't mind. And sometimes I changed the names to protect the innocent. The innocent? But without your stories—and your willingness to share—this book would never have been written. By combining our ideas and creativity, we can provide a valuable resource for parents wanting to give their children quality training.

And to my computer for not dying any sooner—and for Aram Pashaian who let me borrow his to finish the book— thanks. How did people ever write books before the days of computers?

My support team deserves special mention. Marijane Wallack, Raylene Phillips, and Debby Hemby—you've been great. Money can't buy the dedication and commitment that you've shown me! I love you!

A hip hip hooray to my crazy and marvelously delightful children, Kim, Kari and Kevin, who have made my job as a parent a truly unforgettable experience. Without you, I'd be unemployed. You've not only given me my career, but you've inspired me to use every ounce of creativity to keep ahead of you—or at least up with you! Thanks for providing such great in-service training.

And most of all, this book would never have been written if I hadn't fallen in love with an amazingly optimistic man— Jan W. He is my source of inspiration. He makes it possible for me to use my God-given potential—and encourages me to give my best. So, Jan, thanks a million. I'm incredibly proud to be your wife!

Now to you, the reader, thanks for picking up this book. I hope that it will give you exactly what you need to take a fresh look at the challenging career of parenting. God has given you His most precious gift—that of a child. My prayer is that after reading these pages, you may tackle your parenting job with new insight, enthusiasm, and creativity. I could not ask for a greater reward.

TABLE OF CONTENTS

PART III: SPECIFIC STRATEGIES FOR CHILD REARING

CHAPTER 1

INTRODUCTION

Child rearing should be the most rewarding, challenging, and enjoyable experience of a lifetime. But too many parents say, "If I had it to do over again I wouldn't have had children," or "I should have known child rearing wasn't going to be easy when it started with something called labor!"

Well, it may start with labor, but the job of being a parent should not be a laborious one of merely trying to cope. Coping is like treading water; you may keep your head above the surface, but you never get anyplace. Coping isn't enough! I want you to be designing your life—creating an environment for you and your growing children that will maximize each person's potential.

Sure, there are going to be hard days when you feel like throwing in the towel and calling it quits. But you'll never succeed that way. Champions don't win every contest. But they do learn from their mistakes, take time to develop new strategies, and come back into the game with renewed determination and a spirit of optimism.

If you've been thinking about resigning, this book will give you the creative strategies that you will need to come back into the "game" of parenting with that renewed determination and optimism. You can do it. You can design innovative techniques of discipline that will encourage your child to be compliant, accept responsibility, and become self-disciplined. You can be a winner—and make your children winners, too.

And the great thing is, you can enjoy the process. Parenting can be fun!

This is not just another one of those "how-to" discipline books that will tell you how to make the punishment fit the crime so the child will determine in his little heart that life is a lot less hassle if he conforms to society—or at least to Mom and Dad's demands.

This book won't just enumerate the pros and cons of applying the "board of education," nor will you learn all the theory and techniques of behavior modification.

This is not a "how-to" book in the usual sense. It's a book about how you can become a creative disciplinarian and get your kids to do what you want them to do without their realizing what you're doing. It's a success "storybook" of parents who have stumbled onto clever disciplinary strategies. And because this book is about successful techniques I have been selective about the personal examples that I chose to relate. For every creative idea that worked, I may have tried a dozen that didn't, but I've chosen not to tell you about my failures! I've probably at times done everything that I warn parents not to do. I certainly haven't been a perfect parent, but I've enjoyed the experience, and I want you to, also.

So, in addition to these clever disciplinary strategies, this book contains the guidelines for making them work for you, too. In this book you will learn:

1. How to prevent misbehavior before you've got to discipline.

2. Innovative ways to divert your child back onto the road to obedience before he gets too far down the path toward destruction.

3. How to use your spontaneous sense—that maternal or paternal instinct—that God gave you, rather than being bogged down with developmental stages and theoretical models that are sometimes difficult to translate into practice.

4. How to playact problems away.

5. How to keep your child wondering where those eyes are

hiding in the back of your head.

6. How to change behavior by meeting your child's needs rather than your own.

7. How to show love to your children while leading them in the way you want them to go. You are going to enjoy this book because it's filled with unbelievable disciplinary techniques that work! How do I know? Because they are all based on true experiences that parents across the country have related to me.

This book will do something for you that no other discipline book has ever done. It will inspire you to apply your highest sense of God-given creativity to the greatest task in the world—that of training a child in the way she should go without torturing her or you in the process. What inspired me to write this book? It was this letter:

Dear Dr. Kuzma:

I have been attending church for the last three months and am convinced that being a Christian is what God wants me to be. I would like to join God's family of believers, but there is one stumbling block—the practice of child abuse among the members.

I see so many parents spanking and threatening their children. Infants on the changing table are swatted for wiggling. Toddlers are yanked out of church and punished for misbehaving. Even older children are the brunt of threats and criticism, jerks, and slaps.

I can understand a parent occasionally getting angry and losing control, but what I see seems deliberate. When I've been bold enough to ask the reason, I have been given, "Spare the rod and spoil the child" as a Biblical justification.

Is that all the Bible says about discipline? Can't you teach the child the way he should go without

physical or psychological harshness and pain?
Sincerely,
Carol

Here is my reply.

Dear Carol:
There is a better way. You can discipline with love. And, yes, the Bible has a lot more to say about discipline than merely using the rod.

Far too many parents, however, feel that their responsibility for disciplining children ends with the administration of corporal punishment. They subscribe to a literal "spare the rod and spoil the child" philosophy for every misdemeanor.

Just now as I searched my Bible for an answer to your question, I discovered an amazing fact: "Spare the rod and spoil the child" just isn't there—at least not in those words. What is shocking is that I, and thousands of others, have been led to believe the opposite.

Yes, there are references to "the rod of correction" (Prov. 10:13; 13:24; 22:15; 23:13, 14; 29:15). But these texts seem to be dealing with hard-core fools, children who rebelliously refuse instruction, who just can't seem to understand milder measures of discipline. The message seems to be: "Punishment that will bring a child to his senses is better than nothing at all." And I agree with that!

I'm not against spanking for willful defiance if the child is old enough to realize he deserves it and young enough not to be humiliated. But I am against inflicting pain on another person just because we're angry, or just because he is misbehaving, when there is a more humane and effective way to teach him appropriate behavior.

As I consider the Biblical "rod of correction," I wonder if God's penmen had in mind something like the shepherd's rod. Do you think good shepherds go around beating their disobedient sheep on their behinds? I hardly think so. When a sheep is about to make a mistake, they press the rod against its side to turn the sheep in the desired direction, or they use the rod to protect the sheep from predators. The rod means security to the little lambs. And if the sheep could talk, I think they would say to the shepherd, "Thy rod and thy staff, they comfort me."

For a balanced picture of Biblical discipline, don't just read the "rod of correction" texts; read the complete Book of Proverbs. You'll be overwhelmed with texts such as "love covers all offenses" and "a soft answer turns away wrath." (Prov. 10:12; 15:1).

Being effective teachers of our children is such an important task that we can't afford to err by only focusing on a few isolated texts. Instead, Christians should follow the counsel to, "Trust in the LORD with all your heart; and lean not on your own understanding; In all your ways acknowledge Him, and He shall direct your paths" (Prov. 3:5-6 NKJV).

Perhaps one of the best ways God has directed us is by giving us the example of His Son. "Let the children come unto me," were the words of a God who lovingly and tenderly taught the ignorant and misbehaving "children" He encountered on earth. He dealt with them in a significantly different way, not the traditional way of treating people as they rightly deserved. He never did anything to alienate a sinner. His understanding promoted a relationship of love and trust.

I can't, in my wildest imagination, see Christ paddling a child, jerking her around or threatening her within an inch of her life. But I can see Him influencing by example, teaching through object lessons and stories, allowing the headstrong to suffer the consequences of their ways and saying with firmness, "No, and I mean it!"

Let's follow Christ's example of being significantly different as we walk among His children. Let's teach them in the same loving, tender way. If we follow His pattern, we should be the most understanding parents on earth!

Carol, this book is for you and all the other Carols of the world who have questioned the harsh, traditional approach to child rearing. May the ideas you find here be meaningful as you search for more rational, effective, and innovative ways to teach your own special children.

Teaching a child in such a way that he grows up to be in favor with God and man, is a tremendous challenge. We must use every bit of the creativity God has given us to be effective. We must learn to prevent problems so they don't grow into unmanageable behaviors requiring radical "surgery"!

If this task seems overwhelming, remember that "all things are possible with God" (Mk 10:27). Let this be your prayer: "Father God: Give me insight into the reasons my child acts as he does. Give me patience and hope to work through the toughest problem. And give me the wisdom to teach my child the way to go—just as You would."

And Carol, welcome to God's family. It's a great place to be. Let's work together to make a little heaven on earth for all God's children.

In His love and for His kids,
Kay Kuzma

PART ONE

CREATIVE DISCIPLINE: BASIC PRINCIPLES

CHAPTER 2

A HUG AND A KISS . . . AND . . .

You opened this book because of the title, didn't you? You could understand a hug and a kiss—but what kind of a book would advocate a "kick in the pants"?

Well, you'll understand better what a "kick in the pants" has to do with discipline after reading this story:

"Kevin, I need your help," I said one hurried morning. "We have fifteen minutes before we have to leave for school and I can't get everything done by myself."

"But I don't want to help."

"Well, what will it take to change your mind?"

"What will you give me?" gleamed nine-year-old Kevin, seeing an opportunity to bargain for something special.

Not wanting to be bribed into promising the moon, I told him I'd give him a hug.

"That's not enough," responded Kevin with visions of sugarplums and dimes dancing before his eyes.

"Okay," I said, willing to bargain. "I'll just have to give you something else."

"What?" replied Kevin eagerly.

"For everything you do for me, I'll not only give you a hug, but I'll also give you a kiss!"

This was not what Kevin wanted—or expected. "Not enough," he said again, shaking his head.

"Well, enough of that sweet stuff!" I thought. "I'll end up bargaining the fifteen minutes away."

"All right," I said, "for everything you do for me I'll give you a hug and a kiss—and a kick in the pants."

"A what?!" he asked startled.

"A kick in the pants," I repeated.

"No," he laughed as he shook his head. "That's still not enough."

"OK, I'll give you something else if you really want it."

"What?" he asked again.

"Well," I hesitated, "I'll give you a hug and a kiss . . . and a kick in the pants and . . . and a nibble on the ear."

He hesitated momentarily as if he couldn't believe this was coming from his mom and then shouted, "I'll take it!"

Eager to see if I'd hold to my bargain he asked, "What shall I do?"

"Make your bed," I directed.

He ran to his room, pulled up the covers, positioned his pillow and smoothed it all out.

"Done," he shouted as he ran to me for his reward. I bent down and kissed him. Then while hugging him tight, I reached around his body with my foot and tapped him on his behind and then tried to nibble his ear.

"Stop," he giggled. "What next?"

"The dirty clothes need to be carried to the laundry room." Off he ran, appearing moments later for a repeat performance.

Wow, did Kevin work. Fifteen minutes of double-time, while I was kept busy hugging, kissing, kicking and nibbling.

Now, I would never suggest that a kick in the pants is the answer for a parent who complains of a child balking when it comes to housework. Nor would I mention hugging, kissing and nibbling. It probably wouldn't work for your child. It may never work again with Kevin. But we sure had a great time with the game while it lasted—and it certainly was effective in getting Kevin to do what needed to be done.

"That's a bunch of nonsense," you say. "You should tell a child once and he jolly well better do it, or else! Parents shouldn't have to play games to get their children to obey."

Maybe not. But life is a whole lot more pleasant if occasionally you do make a game out of it.

This is just one example of how creativity won the day. Yes, it's true that most parents threaten and shout when a child hesitates to obey. But that only makes the discipline task distasteful to both young and old. If the same lesson of obedience can be taught in a clever, fun-loving way, why not?

I challenge you to be significantly different—to be creative.

Note: To avoid the continual use of *he* and *him* to refer to any child, I have alternated the use of masculine and feminine pronouns throughout the book.

CHAPTER 3

THE STRING STRATEGY

Children are born with a will that must be molded. But some people believe that children are also born either compliant or defiant. I don't believe that. Rather, I believe children are born with varied characteristics, some of which are easier to live with than others.

When a number of more difficult characteristics are seen in the personality and behavior of your child, the tendency is to try to force him into behaving more like the "perfect" child you want him to be. The more you push your expectations upon him, rather than respecting his God-given characteristics, the more resistant he becomes to change—and the more defiant.

I believe parents may be the cause of much of the defiant behavior in children. I can best illustrate what I mean with a string, because children are like strings.

Take a string and stretch it out in front of you. Now take one end and push the string forward—against itself. Does the string move straight in the direction you're pushing? No, of course not. It wrinkles up. And if you keep pushing you will soon have a wadded-up string. But try pulling the string in the way you want it to go and it will follow.

Children are like strings; they tend to resist when they feel pushed or forced into doing something. Once they start to resist, the tendency of most parents is to push them all the more, to threaten, to manipulate, to force, and to punish.

And the consequence is, the more you push, the more rebellious the child becomes.

There may be times when you think pushing or forcing a child results in compliance. But in too many cases it's like the little boy whose dad told him to sit down in church. When the boy kept jumping up, his dad physically pushed the kid into his seat with the command, "I said SIT DOWN!" The little boy sat there, but a few minutes later you could hear him muttering, "I may be sitting on the outside, but I'm standing on the inside!"

Outward compliance caused by forcing doesn't necessarily mean inner compliance, and sooner or later inner defiance causes outward defiance!

The key to diminishing a child's stubborn resistance is to remember just how much children and strings are alike. If you push them in the direction you want them to go, they won't do it.

Using the String Strategy—not pushing the child but leading him—should begin at birth by respecting the child's rights as a human being. Don't rudely interrupt a baby by snatching away a rattle, sticking a bottle in her mouth, or picking her up as if she were a rag doll and had no feelings. Don't impose your will on the baby just because she has no choice.

Instead, slow down. Observe your baby. If she is interested in something, respect that. Talk to her even though she can't answer yet. When you must pick her up, you could say, "Are you ready to go with Mommy? I'll pick you up now."

Prepare your infant for changes you are going to be imposing on her. Get her attention. Tell her what you are going to do. If it's changing diapers, keep up a running commentary on your actions and this will capture her full attention. You'll notice the wiggling—the resistance—will disappear! Then say, "Thank you for being so cooperative," and reward her for compliance. Give her an extra snuggle and kiss. Rewarding the child for compliance is a lot better than forcing your will on her and then having to punish her for defiance.

If you show genuine respect, you will have a much better chance of winning your child's cooperation from day one. I challenge you to try it. See if it doesn't make a difference!

As children grow older, how should stubborn resistance be handled? Go back to the string. If you want that string to move in a certain direction, don't push it. Take the opposite end and pull—I mean lead—and the string will follow!

Any time a child begins to resist, even slightly, remember the string and immediately quit pushing. Instead, step back a few paces and consider creative ways to lead your child in the direction you want him to go. Respect your child's rights, but don't let him step on yours. As a member of your family and as a citizen, he has certain responsibilities. Your job is to motivate, encourage, guide, and gently influence your child so he will choose to fulfill those responsibilities and do what you want him to do.

And what if he doesn't choose to obey? Well, that's where consequences come in—and all the other creative disciplinary techniques that make up the rest of this book. But, in most cases, if you don't get into a "tug of wills," your child will come around to your way of thinking, or you will reach an acceptable compromise. Keep your emotions under control and take the necessary time to resolve the conflict.

Motivating, encouraging, guiding, and influencing does take time, but it's worth it in order to have the child willingly comply with your requests rather than stubbornly resist everything you say or make decisions based on an attitude of rebellion. Willful defiance too often leads to experimentation with harmful practices, such as smoking pot, using drugs, participating in premarital sex, or running away from home. A rebellious child thinks he is hurting you by his defiant behavior, but in reality he is hurting himself far more!

So, don't push the string. Instead, here are some ways to lead your child in the way you want him to go:

1. Make requests only when your child is not deeply absorbed in some favorite activity. Children don't like to be

interrupted any more than adults do.

2. Give your child fair warning that a change is about to take place. "You have ten minutes before you need to put away your blocks. I'll set the timer."

3. Ask for cooperation: "I really need your help to set the table."

4. When possible, give the child a choice: "I've listed three things that have to be done before we go shopping. Which task would you rather do?"

5. Work together happily. Children enjoy doing what you're doing—if you're fun to be around.

6. Use humor and playacting to hurdle potential conflicts. Play beauty shop when combing tangled hair. Play restaurant with finicky eaters. Reverse your roles when the house needs cleaning—and let the child tell you what to do. (For more ideas, see the chapter entitled "Play Problems Away.")

7. Encourage! Encourage! Encourage! Remember, it's a discouraged child that most often misbehaves. You can turn defiance into compliance if you just remember the String Strategy!

CHAPTER 4

APPLYING THE LOVE CUP PRINCIPLE

Children cannot live without love. During World War II studies of babies in orphanages found that some children failed to develop properly. After a year or two some children were not sitting or walking, and some even died. Why? They had enough food, each one had a crib, and their diapers were changed regularly. But one essential ingredient for growth was missing. No one touched, cuddled, or rocked them. Nobody loved them. Their love cups were empty.

Love is essential for a child's healthy development. It's also important for changing negative behavior into positive behavior. In fact, sometimes love is a more effective behavior changer than discipline!

The Love Cup principle explains why this is so. Your child is like a cup. When she is filled to overflowing she has enough love to give away, she can be loving to you and others, and she will tend to behave in an acceptable manner.

Children equate love and attention. So when your child feels empty, he will try to fill himself with attention, and too often his bid for attention results in obnoxious behavior. Parents generally interpret this negative behavior as something that deserves punishment. But if your child's misbehavior is caused by an empty love cup, punishment will be ineffective. His need for love must first be satisfied.

You have the power to change your child's misbehavior by simply filling his love cup. The story of Lori illustrates how the Love Cup principle works in practice.

Seven-year-old Lori was having a miserable day. She whined, pouted, pushed her little sister, Lisa, and then grabbed away Lisa's favorite doll.

Finally, Mother could stand it no longer. "Lori, what has gotten into you? You'd better straighten up and be kind to your sister, or you're going to get it!"

Lori paid no attention to the threat and continued to say mean things to Lisa. At bedtime Mother told Lori that her words were so sour that she felt like making Lori suck a lemon so she could understand just how sour they were. That made Lori even more angry. "You like Lisa more than you like me," Lori retorted. She fell asleep sulking.

The next morning Lori woke up in a bad mood. She complained miserably when Mother attempted to comb out the tangles in her hair. Mother was beside herself; what was wrong with Lori?

Then she remembered the book *Filling Your Love Cup* that she had read not long ago. Could Lori be suffering from a lack of positive attention? Mother called, "Lori, I think I know what's wrong with you."

"You do?" Lori looked puzzled.

"Yes," said her mother, "your love cup is empty! Come over here and let me fill it up."

Mom sat Lori on her lap and hugged and kissed her and told her how special she was. Lori was surprised, but she obviously enjoyed the attention. She knew she deserved the opposite. After a minute, Mom asked Lori if her love cup was filled.

"No, but it's up to here," said Lori, as she pointed to her chest.

Mother loved her up again. Then she asked, "Is it full now?"

"No," said Lori, "but it's up to my chin."

"Good," said Mother, with a big hug. "Let's see if we can't get that cup so full that it will spill right over the top."

Finally, with a big smile on her face, Lori said that she was full and running over.

"Well, if you've got that much love," said Mother, "why don't you give some of it to your sister?"

"Oh, no," said Lori, "Lisa will just push me away." Mother knew that after the obnoxious way Lori had treated Lisa, that just might happen. But she encouraged Lori to try. Somewhat hesitantly, Lori went up to Lisa and said, "Lisa, I love you," and gave her a hug. Lisa hugged her sister back, real tight. Then they both headed off hand in hand to the breakfast table.

But that's not the end of the story. A few weeks later, Mother had a terrible day. She grumbled and spoke harshly to the girls. After a while, Lori said, "Mommy, I think I know what's wrong with you. Your love cup is empty!" Then she threw her arms around her mom's neck and gave her a big kiss. Do you know what happened to Mother's love cup? Just like that, it filled to overflowing and Mom was her happy self again.

Meeting a child's need for positive attention is the most basic way to both prevent and solve behavior problems. Noted child psychiatrist Rudolf Dreikurs in his book *Children: The Challenge* suggests that attention is the number one reason why children misbehave. When a child's need for attention is not met positively, she will continue to misbehave, and chances are this will lead to the second reason for misbehavior—a struggle for power between the child and authority figures.

The majority of a child's "healthy" misbehavior occurs on these two planes, starting with a need for attention and moving into a need for power and control. Creative disciplinarians will continually work with their children in these areas to keep them from moving on to more pathological misbehavior caused by wanting revenge and feeling inadequate or inferior.

Because the need for attention is the basic cause of misbehavior, creative disciplinarians must be masters at recognizing when their child's love cup is empty, and be willing to fill it immediately. Full cups mean behavior problems are kept to a minimum. But when empty, children try to fill themselves by trying to get more attention. They seek approval; they try to be good. But how often do good children get much attention? Not often. Most children find that they get more attention by being bad, by showing off, acting silly, being destructive, or getting into mischief. Getting attention sometimes becomes such an overwhelming need that children cease to care if it is positive or negative. Being yelled at or beaten is better than being ignored.

I hope your child doesn't have to misbehave in order to get your attention. But has something like this ever happened to you? You just got home from work. It's been a hard day. You're exhausted. You kick off your shoes, flop down on the couch, and begin leafing through the paper. You're particularly interested in what happened on the stock market during the day. Just as you begin to scan the columns, your little three year old comes running up to you saying, "Daddy, Daddy, come outside and see what I made."

What do you do? Say, "Sure, honey, I'll be glad to," and then you put your shoes back on and follow your child outside? Is that what you would do? Not if you're like most parents! Most of us would say something like this, "Not now, Buster, can't you see I'm reading the paper?"

And what does your child do? Retreat and silently wait for you to finish the paper? No, this is the typical scenario . . .

"Daddy, please, I can't wait! I want to show you . . . "

"Well, you jolly well better wait because I'm busy."

"Daddy, let me show you," your child pleads, taking hold of the edge of the paper and wiggling it.

"Let go of the paper! I can't read with you jerking it up and down. Now get out of here and let me finish."

"But, Daddy . . . "

You cut off his pleading by saying, "If you don't give me a

little peace and quiet then I'll give you just what you deserve. Out with you."

And with the threat of impending danger, your child retreats to the other room. But only for a few minutes.

The child hasn't seen you all day and his love cup is almost empty. Since children equate love with attention, the child isn't satisfied until he gets the attention he needs so desperately. So what does Buster do? Well, he takes a flying leap and jumps right into the middle of the paper, tearing it up.

Now what do you do? Give him what he richly deserves? Or do you give him what he so urgently needs?

Most of us just don't understand the subtle (and sometimes not too subtle) messages that our children are trying to give us. Most of us would see this obnoxious behavior of a child as just an ornery streak that needs to be corrected with punishment, when the real message was, "Daddy, my love cup is empty and needs to be filled with a little positive attention— and this can't wait!"

So be prepared. The next time you're reading the paper and your little one comes up and needs a little extra attention, put your paper down, take your child on your lap, or go see what the child wants you to see. Chances are that in a couple of minutes your child's love cup will be full once again with enough positive attention so that he'll say to you, "Okay, Daddy, you can go back and read your paper again." I'll guarantee that you'll enjoy that stock market report a whole lot more by giving love and attention first. And you won't have to put up with an obnoxious child.

Remember the Love Cup principle the next time someone you know becomes obnoxious. When her cup is empty, nothing will change that offensive behavior quite as quickly as a little extra love—positive attention. Spend some fun time together, encourage your child, or share some words of appreciation. See if it doesn't make a difference and reduce your child's need for negative behavior.

One young mother learned about the Love Cup principle at

one of my seminars. She remained skeptical, but her five-year-old David was so unruly she was desperate, ready to try anything. So for a few weeks she patiently filled his love cup. The change was nearly miraculous! David didn't become an angel; he was still an active five year old. But his rebellion disappeared. Gradually he became a happy, responsive, cooperative child.

But David's mother found a new conflict. Her revised child-rearing method caused a problem with her own parents. They disapproved. They subscribed literally to the idea of "spare the rod and spoil the child." Slowly she reverted to her old habits: yelling and spanking. David responded in kind, reverting to his old self: obstinate, challenging, and disagreeable.

Later, David's mother reviewed the seminar material and decided the Love Cup principle was worth another try. In two weeks she wrote to me: "It works. Love really works. My happy, gentle, and fun-loving boy is back again. I'll never again let anyone talk me into emptying his love cup."

The Love Cup principle will work with your child, too. I know it will. Won't you give it a try? I have a feeling someone in your life could use a little filling right now!

CHAPTER 5

THREE BASIC COMMANDMENTS

M ost children grow up with 9,528 rules that cover every minor infraction. But what good are rules if the child can't remember them? If you've ever heard your child say, "But Dad, I don't remember you ever telling me that," then chances are you've given your child more rules than he can remember. Rules alone don't make well-disciplined children!

It's easy to fall into the trap of having too many rules. Here is how it happens: Babies can't generalize that if touching the knobs on the TV is wrong, so is touching the stereo knobs. They must be carefully taught every specific thing you don't want them to do. You quickly learn to say "no" to each questionable situation or behavior since this is the only effective way to teach babies. Without thinking, you continue making up more and more rules until you have made so many rules for your children to obey that even you can't remember them all!

If a child tries to operate on rules alone, here is what happens: A questionable situation comes up and Betty needs to decide what to do. She flips through her mental rule book. If she can't remember a rule against it, then she decides it must be okay and she goes ahead and does what she wants. If it turns out to be wrong and her parents ask, "Why did you do it?" the child often blames them. "You never told me not to!" Or if there was an already established rule, she simply says, "I forgot!"

Just making up more rules is never going to help your child learn what's right and wrong. If he is not clear on what makes a behavior right or wrong, then he'll never be able to make wise decisions on his own.

So, throw away your rule book. Instead, establish three basic commandments as the code of behavior for your children—and YOU! Here they are:

1. You may not hurt yourself.
2. You may not hurt others.
3. You may not hurt things. These three basic commandments cover an abundance of misbehavior, allowing the child the necessary framework for making decisions. Without these three rules, kids can make some pretty foolish decisions. For example, Jack wants to play baseball in your front yard. He checks the old rule book and can't remember whether you have ever said, "No baseball in the front yard." He does recall that rule #5422 says, "No football in the garden." That's close, but this is the front yard not the garden, and it's baseball not football. So he calls, "Batter up," without ever thinking about the picture window a few yards away!

But if he would apply the three commandments to this situation, then he would ask, "Will playing baseball in the front yard hurt me? No. Will it hurt others? No. Will it hurt things? Oh, oh, there is the picture window. It could easily get broken. I guess I had better not play baseball in the front yard."

Start teaching these unbreakable commandments by tagging them on to more specific limits. You might say, "No playing in the street, because you may not hurt yourself." "I can't let you hit your brother, because you may not hurt others." "No jumping on the beds because you may not hurt things."

I don't want you to get the idea that these three commandments are only effective for the younger set. They can continue to be effective throughout the growing years. Here are some examples of things you might tell your teenager:

"No, I can't let you sit out in the car and neck. Emotions can easily get out of hand and lead to a sexual encounter. I don't want you doing anything that might ultimately hurt yourself or someone else."

"You won't be able to go to the game until your homework is done. Grades are important if you want to get that state scholarship, and I can't let you do anything that might hurt yourself."

"John, you'll have to change shoes before playing ball on the lawn. Cleats are too hard on the new grass, and I can't let you hurt things."

If you are consistent in applying these three commandments to the various limits in your home, it won't take long for your children to get the idea. The more often you remind them of these commandments in the early years, the sooner they will start applying them to the decisions they make about what they should or should not do. And when this happens, you will find your job as the family disciplinarian a whole lot easier.

CHAPTER 6

CATEGORIZING KIDS' BEHAVIOR

I doubt if it will surprise you if I tell you that you can't teach your child everything at once. If you try, you will be constantly nagging, and the consequence of this is not very pleasant. In the first place, you'll become negative and frustrated and miss the joy of parenting. Second, you'll make your child's life miserable. Most children can only take pushy parents so long before they end up rebelling. Some rebel openly by refusing to obey and by acting out their anger in destructive or hurtful ways. Others try to get back at you by resorting to passive aggression. In other words, they "win" by doing annoying things behind your back or by just refusing to listen or act on what you say. Laziness or dawdling, for example, may be a symptom of passive aggression.

But the biggest consequence of trying to teach your child everything at once is that you'll be so busy correcting the minor infractions that you may not have the energy or time to deal with the major ones—the behavior that violates one of the three basic commandments of not hurting yourself, others, or things. If this happens, the child begins to feel that these commandments are really not so important after all, and he loses respect for your authority.

Therefore, you must decide what is really important to you at this time and concentrate on teaching those things. Once those lessons are learned, you can move on to secondary matters. I've found it helps to begin by dividing your child's behavior into three categories.

Category 1: Behavior you approve of and would like to see more often. Your list might include such things as: being polite, sharing toys, sorting the dirty clothes, playing quietly while baby naps, etc.

Category 2: Behavior that you can't allow because it breaks one of the three basic commandments of hurting yourself, others, or things. This list might include: standing up in the bathtub, biting siblings, or throwing things in the house.

Category 3: Behavior that you may not like, but you can live with! This will probably be your longest list. Category 3 behaviors might include such things as: making "lumpy" beds with the sheet hanging below the bedspread, using a thumb to push the last bite on the fork, leaving the bathroom mirror spotted or showering for 15 minutes when 5 is sufficient.

Once you have categorized your child's behaviors then your plan of action is simple.

For Category 1: Reward the behavior you approve.

For Category 2: Correct the behavior you can't allow.

For Category 3: Either ignore the things you may not like but can tolerate or creatively teach the child more appropriate behavior without her knowing what's happening. The creative discipline techniques in this book are extremely effective when dealing with Category 3 behavior.

Your first step in dealing with Category 3 behavior is to prioritize these behaviors according to how badly they bother you. You must decide what's really important to deal with NOW. Making the bed may be important, but not as important as brushing teeth and saying, "please." Therefore, concentrate on toothbrushing and saying "please." Once these become habitual, you can move on to creatively teach other behaviors.

Carefully monitor yourself—and your child. If you notice you are correcting more than you are rewarding, something is wrong. Delay trying to change some of those Category 3 behaviors and concentrate on what's really important NOW. Don't fall into the trap of being a negative parent. Enjoy yourself. Parenting should be fun!

And watch your child. If you notice a cloud of negativism come over his usually sunny attitude and if you begin to detect some subtle resistance to your suggestions, it just may be you're pushing or correcting too much. It's a lot better to back off for a while and re-establish a positive relationship with your child than to blindly push on and take the chance of ending up with a rebellious child sometime in the future.

CHAPTER 7

TEACHING
EASY OBEDIENCE

I believe in having a good time with children, but that doesn't mean I'm indifferent to misbehavior or am afraid to lay down the law if necessary. Quite the opposite. The creative approach to discipline only works if parents are strong enough to establish, maintain, and enforce limits. Only then will children feel secure in their environment and respect the adult enough to willingly obey.

Teaching children to obey doesn't have to be a tiresome task. It can be fun. However, you can't laugh, play games, and joke with your children and expect obedience unless you establish certain ground rules—a code of behavior by which they must live.

Obedience is the most important lesson a child must learn—so it's absolutely necessary that you make the lesson easy. Make it fun. Find subtle ways to encourage, influence and motivate your child to live within the limits. Make it worthwhile for your child to obey. Sure, it's human nature to test the limits occasionally, and kids wouldn't be kids if they didn't. But your goal is to establish within your children a basic willingness to obey. And your success depends on you—their first and most important teacher!

The first essential factor in teaching children obedience is to establish their respect for your authority by making sure you enforce your requests consistently.

In the early months and years, you must teach your children that "father or mother knows best." They must learn to trust you to make wise decisions for them when they are too young or immature to know what's good for themselves. This is the time to establish your credibility as an expert decision maker, an authority. The longer you wait to teach this lesson, the harder it will be for your child to learn.

For many people the word "authority" conjures up images of judges, rulers, or policemen—those with the power to enforce unpleasant rules and regulations. But an authority is also a specialist, a wise person, an expert. This is the kind of authority you must strive to become as a parent. Your children should obey you because they trust your wisdom and expertise, not because they fear your superior power or strength.

The first few years of your child's life is the time to convey the message of your authority. To do this you must enforce your instructions and requests immediately. However, make sure that your instructions are enforceable. Too many parents go about teaching the obedience lesson all wrong, trying to enforce the unenforceable. For example: "Stop crying. Now, I'll have no more of that. If you don't stop crying this instant, I'll give you something to cry about!" Sound familiar? Or this, "Eat those vegetables. I said eat them—don't you dare spit them out."

Parents have also been heard saying such things as, "If I've told you once, I've told you a million times, go to sleep!" Or in the struggle of trying to get a child toilet trained, they may demand, "No more wetting your pants. You're a big boy. Use the toilet!"

Well, if you're like most parents, I bet you've gone through hassles like trying to get your children to stop crying, eat their dinner, go to sleep, or go to the bathroom in the proper place. It's not that the requests are wrong; it's just that they may be given prematurely, before you've taught your child that you are the authority—a respected authority!

These types of requests can't be enforced. You can shout

until you're blue in the face, threaten, and bribe—but if the child really doesn't want to do it, he has ultimate control of his crying, eating, sleeping, and eliminating. Therefore, these requests are almost impossible to enforce. So don't start there. Start with requests that are realistic—requests that you can enforce. For example:

"Come inside." (Go out and bring your child in.)

"Turn off the TV." (Take your little one to the TV and help her turn it off.)

"Don't hit your brother." (Separate them.)

"Wash your face and hands." (Lead your child to the basin and hand him soap and a washcloth.)

"Button your shirt." (Help him button it.)

"Put your bike away." (Take your child by the hand and lead her to the bicycle. Help her put it away.)

When your child has learned to be obedient to the requests that you are able to enforce, then because he respects you, he will be more willing to obey requests that you can't really enforce because of the child's control over his own body functions or emotions.

Once you have decided that you can enforce a certain request, here is the procedure to follow:

1. Make the request once and be sure that the child hears and understands.

2. If the child responds positively, reward her with a word of appreciation at the feeling level: "I feel happy when you do what I ask," or with a special demonstration of love, like a hug or a smile.

3. If your child doesn't respond, repeat the request as you begin to enforce it. For example, "I asked you to come into the house for supper." Then do whatever is necessary to get her willing compliance. For example, make a game of getting to the house. "I bet I can beat you to the back door!" "Let's guess how many steps it will take to get to your chair at the table!" You might want to take the child's hand and skip to the door.

When you enforce a request or limit, there is no need to be harsh and punitive. Your words and actions should convey two important messages: You expect obedience, and you will interrupt whatever you are doing to enforce your request.

Beware of distraction techniques that your child may try to use to get out of having to obey or to delay obedience. "It isn't my turn to empty the trash." "I did it last time." "It isn't fair." Even "I love you, Mommy," or "What time is it?" can be attempts at distraction. Many parents fall right into the child's trap and their request gets sidetracked while they engage in trying to convince Junior that it is his turn, that the request is fair, or whatever. Distraction techniques should be totally ignored—not discussed at all—until the request is obeyed. Simply repeat your request again after each distraction technique is used.

Mom: "Empty the trash."

Junior: "It's too hard."

Mom: "Empty the trash."

Junior: "Why do I have to do it right now?"

Mom: "Empty the trash."

Junior: "I had to do it last time. You're mean."

Mom: "Empty the trash."

Junior: "When can I go out to play?"

Mom: "Empty the trash." Do you get the idea? You may sound like a broken record, but once your child discovers that distraction techniques don't work, obedience comes much easier.

You must also remember to not hide your request in the middle of irrelevant verbiage. "Danny, please hang up all the clothes that are on your bedroom floor," is much better than, "Danny, why are you so sloppy? If I've told you once I've told you a hundred times to pick up the clothes on your bedroom floor. Now do it and no more dilly dallying or you'll be sorry." It's easy for a request to be lost in the middle of many words.

Vera was entertaining company. Her four-year-old son was playing with the kitten in a rough manner. "Sean," his mother said calmly, "pet the kitten softly. Don't pull its tail." Sean acted as if he hadn't heard and continued mauling the cat. Vera went over to Sean and said, "Sean, I said to pet the kitten softly, and I meant what I said. Please hand me the kitten." At that Sean exploded, threw the kitten across the room, and ran for dear life to his room, thinking he'd be safe there since Mom was entertaining company and would be too involved to discipline him.

But Vera knew better than to allow such disrespectful behavior to go undisciplined. She excused herself from her guests and explained, "I'm sorry I must leave you alone now, but I must talk to Sean. I don't know how long I will be, but I can't let this behavior go undisciplined." She then left her company, opened Sean's door, and sat down on his bed. Sean was lying down with his face buried in his pillow. Mom began to rub his back and for two or three minutes nothing was said. Vera knew that her words would be wasted if Sean's emotions were too strong to allow her to reason with him. Finally, Sean could stand the silence no longer. "Did the company leave?"

"No," replied his mom.

"Then what are you doing in here?"

"I can't let you get away with such disrespectful behavior. My most important job is to teach you how to behave appropriately. You are much more important to me than my guests." Then Vera went on to talk to him about how unacceptable his behavior had been. They both decided an appropriate consequence would be for Sean to stay in his room for a while. And if it ever happened again a spanking would be appropriate.

After about 15 minutes the problem appeared to be settled, and Mom went back to her guests. Surprisingly, they didn't mind her absence. In fact, they respected Vera for putting the training of her child first. But more important, Sean never forgot the fact that his mother, no matter how busy and occupied, was never too busy to discipline him.

It takes time to consistently enforce your requests. But if

you're inconsistent, then all you can expect of your child is a 50/50 compliance rate.

Let's pretend that Mom thinks it is very important for Junior to make his bed each morning. He knows exactly how she feels—it is a rule that he should obey. But Mom is very busy during the morning hours and often forgets to check his room. When she does check and finds an unmade bed, she sometimes feels that it's easier to ignore the infraction than to exert the extra effort needed to get him to make his bed before the school bus arrives. So she decides to wait until after school. Then, by the time they both get home, the bed is forgotten.

Now, Mom still feels very strongly about the bed, and she has communicated this to Junior in no uncertain terms. Shouldn't this be enough to get the job done? He clearly knows what he should do. Why doesn't he do it? The reason is that this requirement has not been consistently enforced.

When you enforce requirements—even very important requirements—inconsistently, your child will become a "50/50" decision maker. This is what happens. Junior wakes up in the morning and yawns. "Let's see," he says as he tumbles out of bed, "shall I make my bed this morning? Well, chances are 50/50 that Mom won't even notice, and I really don't feel like doing it. So . . . I think I'll take a chance and leave it unmade."

If Mom would consistently enforce and reinforce the type of behavior she expected from her child until this behavior became ingrained and habitual, the scenario would be different. Junior would wake up in the morning and say, "Let's see, shall I make my bed?" Then he would weigh the alternatives ("If I don't, Mom will make me do it before breakfast") and make a wise decision ("I guess I'd better do it and get it over with").

Children will abide by reasonable requirements and limitations, but their tendency is to do as little as possible. Even a two year old will try to get away with as much as she can.

41

She'll quickly learn that even though her parents say "no," frequently the limits will come tumbling down if she kicks hard enough. When her persistent challenging meets with parenting inconsistency, she'll be encouraged to kick at every limit she would just as soon do without.

It is particularly difficult to be consistent when Dad, Mom, Grandpa, Cousin Joe, Aunt Bessie and the baby-sitter are all involved in parenting. When there are several parenting figures, the child often becomes frustrated by conflicting messages. A child will take full advantage of this opportunity and play one adult against another in order to get his own way. A child does not have to take lessons to learn how to divide and conquer! Agreeing on what the limits for a child should be and then consistently enforcing them will convince your child that he can't get away with disobedience.

Teaching your child to be obedient to authority is probably the most important lesson of early childhood. By making sure your request has been heard and understood, by rewarding the child for responding positively, and by immediately and consistently enforcing your requests, your child should have no trouble learning that you mean what you say.

Remember, just ask your child to do one thing, and then make sure you follow through. This is the first step in teaching obedience.

CHAPTER 8

SETTING OBEYABLE LIMITS

Obedience is the willingness to live within the limits that have been established by others. We find limits on every level of society, and we can quickly get into hot water by ignoring them. The sooner your child can learn the importance of obeying limits, the happier he will be—and the more fulfilling your job as a parent will be. "Children, obey your parents" (Eph 6:1) is wise counsel. Why is it that some children have such a difficult time obeying?

The best preparation for you in understanding why your child may or may not be obeying is to think carefully about your own attitudes toward limits or laws. Why do you choose to abide by some? Why do you ignore others? Take the speed limit, for example. Every day you must choose whether or not to be obedient. I have a feeling that almost all parents who drive have been guilty of exceeding the limit at one time or another. Many drivers do it daily! What affects your choice? Would you go over the 55-mile-per-hour speed limit if you knew your car would blow up at 56 MPH? None of us would! In fact, most of us wouldn't get near the limit—many of us wouldn't get near the car! The consequence would be too severe.

Now pretend that the only thing that would happen if you exceeded the speed limit would be a flag popping out of the hood of your car announcing to the world, "I'm speeding." And let's say that the only way you could get the flag back down would be to have a policeman give you a ticket and wind it down with a special tool. Would you still go over 55?

Some might, especially if they were rushing to the hospital or to catch a plane. The consequence would not be that severe. But it would keep most of us on the straight and narrow. We would be embarrassed if other people saw our flag, and since we don't like paying fines, we would choose to stay within the limit.

But, what if everyone was driving around with their flags flying? Chances are you would, too. It's very tempting to disregard the limits when everyone else is, also.

When the speed limit is unclear, it's easy to ignore or take our chances of not being caught. In some states there is no consequence until excessive speeds are reached. But traveling through the state of Ohio where the costly consequence for the slightest infraction is clearly posted, I noticed that a lot more drivers were obeying the limit. I was, too!

Children react to limits the same way adults do. If the consequence is severe enough to be meaningful, they will be obedient. If they are afraid of the social consequences of disobedience, they will comply. But if the consequence is insignificant and everyone else is ignoring the limits, they will take their chances. And when the limit is unclear—if one thing is stated but there is no consequence for slight infractions or if there is inconsistent enforcement of the limits—then kids will not only bounce up against the limits, but more often than not will bounce right through them.

Here is a checklist of questions to ask yourself in determining if a limit is "obeyable."

1. Is the limit clear? When you ask your child to mow the lawn, what do you mean? Do you mean that in addition to mowing the lawn, the grass clippings need to be raked into piles and bagged for the trash? Do you want your child to also use the edger? Do you expect the cuttings on the walk to be swept away? If so, be sure to state that exactly.

2. When do you expect obedience? Is the time limit clear?

Is it reasonable to both you and your child? Does your child agree to this time limit?

3. Is the consequence for disobedience severe enough to be meaningful? Have you stated the consequence clearly? If you are not yet sure what the consequence should be, have you at least made sure your child knows there will be one? Are you prepared to follow through with imposing the consequence?

4. Is the social pressure such that obedience is possible? Or are other children disobeying the limit, making it more difficult for your child to comply? On the other hand, is there a possibility for social acceptance if the limit is obeyed or social embarrassment if it is not?

5. Does your child understand your limit? Can your child tell you in her own words what she understands the request to be? Have you written it down so she can read it?

If you don't want your child bouncing through your limits, then you've got to make it very clear that you mean what you say. Here's how one clever mother taught her child the importance of staying within the limits with a quadruple ice-cream cone.

Mom wanted four-year-old Terry to clean his room. She knew it was important to make her request very specific so he would know exactly what she was requiring. She also wanted to establish how long he had to get the job done.

So, after getting Terry's attention, she said, "Terry, I want you to clean your room. That means make your bed, pick up the blocks on the floor and put them where they belong on the shelf."

To make sure he was listening she asked him to repeat what she had said. Then she added, "And I will give you exactly one hour to finish the job. That's 60 minutes—not 61. If you are not finished in 60 minutes there will be a consequence. Do you understand?"

Again Terry repeated what Mom had said and helped set the buzzer that was to ring in 60 minutes. "And Terry," she added, "I'm not going to remind you as I've done in the past.

This time it's up to you to do what I've asked you. But remember, if it's not done, there WILL be a consequence."

The clock began ticking. Thirty minutes went by, then 45. Still Terry had not started on his room. As the buzzer was about to ring, Mom realized that Terry wasn't going to make it and she would have to impose some kind of consequence. She thought of spanking. That would cause pain, but had nothing to do with his ignoring the limits. What about withholding privileges? That didn't seem to fit either. How could she teach him the lesson that she meant what she said?

A crazy idea popped into her head. The buzzer rang. Terry had bounced through the limit. The bed was still unmade, and he hadn't started picking up the blocks. "Good-bye, Terry," she called. "I'm leaving for the ice-cream shop."

Terry's ears pricked up. "Just a minute, I'm coming."

"Oh, no, you're not!" Mom said firmly. "You had 60 minutes to clean your room and you didn't do it. So the consequence for not obeying is no ice cream. You have to stay here with Dad."

Terry couldn't believe his mommy would actually go to the ice-cream shop without him. But truth dawned when Mom came home with a quadruple ice-cream cone, sat down in front of Terry and ate the whole thing herself.

Do you know what happened the next time Mom said, "Clean your room. You have 60 minutes"? Terry had the room spick-and-span in about 5 minutes. And that one time, Mom rewarded Terry by taking him out for ice cream.

It's important not to get into the habit of rewarding children for everything you ask them to do. You must be especially careful about using sweets as a reward. But in this case, it only took one ice-cream cone for Terry to learn the lesson that Mom meant what she said. And learning that you mean what you say is such an important lesson that if it can be taught with one ice-cream cone then I think it's well worth it. The quadruple ice-cream cone made the lesson easy and fun. Anytime you can do that, you've got a winner!

CHAPTER 9

LETTING THEM LIVE WITH THE CONSEQUENCES

Billy goofed around after school and got home late. He missed going to the basketball game with his friends—they just couldn't wait.

Sue planted a garden for her school project and forgot to water it. Everything died and she received an F on the project.

Jim left his good mitt out on the lawn overnight. The automatic sprinkler system came on and by morning the mitt was a soggy mess. Jim missed a fly ball to left field in the championship game that afternoon and the other team won because the mitt he had to borrow wasn't familiar.

And Terry didn't clean his room in the allotted 60 minutes, so he couldn't go out for ice cream with Mom.

Consequences. They often seem so harsh. Why didn't Billy's Mom try to find him after school so he could see his favorite team play? Why didn't Dad water Sue's garden when he saw the radishes drooping? Why didn't Jim's parents remind him to bring in his mitt? It was an expensive loss.

Why? Because these parents had wisely learned that one of the best techniques for modifying a child's behavior is to let her suffer the consequences of her inappropriate behavior—to learn from her mistakes. Consequences are especially effective when milder measures, such as reminding or warning a child, have failed to produce behavior changes. Letting a child suffer the consequences is the quickest and, in the long run,

47

the most painless way to encourage a child to make wise decisions.

If children don't understand the link between their actions and certain consequences, they may feel they can get by with whatever they choose. Delinquents, for example, are sometimes surprised when their unlawful behavior finally results in a prison sentence.

"Why me?" they question.

"Why? Because you broke the law!"

"Sure I broke the law. I've been breaking laws all my life and nothing has ever happened before. Why now?"

It seems incredible to us that kids think they can disobey certain laws and never have to pay the consequences. But just ask teenagers in trouble, and in most cases you will find that they thought they could get by with it—probably because they always had before.

The only way kids are ever going to feel responsible for their behavior is to allow them to suffer from the consequences, no matter how painful it may sometimes be to both parents and kids. If parents keep bailing them out of the little messes they get themselves into, chances are they'll think they can get out of the big ones, too. And they never will learn responsibility.

Consequences come in two types: Natural ones, and those that are imposed by parents or some other authority figure.

Natural consequences happen automatically if the child continues on his own path of "destruction." For example, the natural consequence of eating green apples might be a stomachache, or the natural consequence of a messy room might be to suffer embarrassment when a teacher comes to visit. Children often learn they'd better not hit others by suffering the natural consequence of getting hit back. Others learn to lock up their bikes because they didn't and their bikes were stolen.

Sometimes the natural consequence can be harmful to children, such as the consequence of being hit by a car when playing in the street or getting burned when experimenting with matches. Parents need to protect children from these terrible consequences, but at the same time teach them to be responsible for their behavior. Other actions (such as not cleaning one's room) don't carry many natural consequences, so the parents have to create them. The way you do this is by imposing a consequence on the child—a logical consequence, so the child gets the message that his punishment is related to his crime.

Some parents find it hard to impose consequences on their children, and consequently children are seemingly getting away with "murder." And their parents end up being the ones who are suffering!

I once read a story to my children that made a deep impression on me. It was about a poor boy and his mother. One day the boy came home with an egg. When his mother asked him where he got it, he honestly said he took it from under the neighbor's chicken. "You mean you stole it?" his mother questioned.

"Not really," the boy reasoned. "I found it, so I figured it was mine."

His mother didn't like the idea of her son taking the egg, but since he was so hungry, she figured one time wouldn't hurt. So she cooked up the egg for his supper and told him to never do it again. Well, do you think this stopped the stealing? Of course not. It just encouraged it. Because he was poor he felt the world owed him nice things, so he took what he wanted. In the end he was imprisoned for embezzlement. Was he sorry? He was sorry he got caught, but not sorry for stealing. He took no responsibility for his actions. Instead, he blamed his mother, "If stealing was so wrong, why didn't you make me return that first egg I stole—and punish me for it?"

If only this mother had imposed the logical consequence and made her son take back the egg. The brief moment of embarrassment it may have caused her son might have saved him from a life of crime and years of punishment. None of us want that to happen to our children, so let's start today to help them link their behavior to consequences. Help your children as early as possible to take responsibility for their behavior so they won't have to suffer for it later.

To be an effective disciplinarian doesn't mean that you have to be always doling out punishment and choice words of wisdom. I've found that some of the biggest lessons my kids have learned were lessons they taught themselves by suffering from the natural consequences of their behavior.

For example, one time when Kim, Kari, and Kevin were preschoolers, they decided to buy their daddy a box of his favorite candy for his birthday. As soon as the decision was made, they were so excited about getting the candy that they wanted to go shopping immediately. So, I drove them to the store. They found the candy box on the shelf and gently carried it to the checkout clerk and started shaking their pennies out of their piggy bank.

At last the candy was purchased and we headed home. I didn't have time to immediately wrap the gift so I put it on the top shelf of the pantry, thinking it would be safe there.

Well, the kids had seen where I put it. And later that afternoon one of them said, "Boy, I bet Daddy's candy is delicious. I wish I could have a piece."

"Me, too," they all agreed. "I bet Daddy wouldn't even know if we took one piece."

So, Kim climbed up on the tall stool and reached for the box of candy. She took out one piece, took off the gold foil, took a bite and started to hand what was left to Kari. "No," said Kari, "I want my own piece."

"Me, too," chimed Kevin. So, Kim took out two more pieces and gave them to Kari and Kevin. She looked at the box and decided no one could tell any candy was missing, so she put it back on the top shelf.

But the next day, they again remembered the candy—and back they went for more. Kim dished out three more pieces. And they kept doing this until the box was empty. But they never said anything to me. So, the day of Jan's birthday I took the box down and wrapped it without realizing what they'd done.

"What's in Daddy's package?" the kids asked when they saw the present.

"The candy you bought for Daddy's birthday," I answered.

"But," gasped the kids, "we can't give Daddy that."

"Why not?" I asked.

"Because, it's empty."

"It's empty?!" I exclaimed.

"Yes," said the kids. "We ate it all up. We'll have to get Daddy some more."

"There isn't time," I explained. "And you don't have any more money. You'll just have to give Daddy an empty birthday present!"

And that's what happened. Jan unwrapped the gift and asked, "What is it?"

"It's an empty birthday present." They hung their heads in embarrassment. "We ate it all up. But we're sorry—and we'll never give you an empty birthday present again!"

They never did!

Now, I could have lectured them about not stealing and about how terrible it was to not have a present for Daddy. I could have sent them to their rooms or even spanked them. And then having punished them for their wrongdoing, I could have gone down and bought another box of candy. But the effect would never have been the same.

It's sometimes difficult to allow your child to experience the natural consequence because "good" parents want the best for their children. I know one mom who gets up early each day to make a lunch for her teenage boy, even though it's his job to make his own. Why? Because she doesn't want him to go hungry. He's not about to put himself out making a lunch when his mom always bails him out. So what should be his responsibility has become hers because she isn't willing to allow him to suffer the consequence of being hungry.

Another mother takes her child to school when his dawdling causes him to miss the school bus. She doesn't want him to be late. Being tardy would reflect on his citizenship grade, and the teachers might question her competence as a mother if she doesn't care enough about her child to get him to school on time. Consequently, Junior misses the school bus more than he makes it. Since Mom is willing to take him, he doesn't need to be responsible.

But "good" parents don't just put on a good front. "Good" parents must sometimes swallow their own sensitivity and pride to allow a child to suffer from her irresponsibility for her own good! This is very hard to do. I know.

I finally decided that the problem of getting Kevin dressed in the morning could only be solved if I was willing for him to wear pajamas to nursery school—if that was what he chose to do. I needed to teach him the lesson that it was his responsibility to get dressed. One day everyone was dressed and ready for breakfast—everyone, that is, except Kevin.

"Kevin, why aren't you dressed?"

"Because," said Kevin, "I was too busy."

"Too busy playing?" asked his dad.

"Oh no, Daddy, too busy building houses and roads with my blocks."

"But Kevin your job is to get dressed the first thing in the morning before you eat. The rule is you can't eat breakfast in pajamas," I added.

"But I'm hungry. Can't I eat in pajamas just once? Please?"

I thought about it for a moment. Breakfast was on the table, and we were all sitting down ready to eat, so I suggested that the family vote on it. Everyone raised their hands in favor of it—Kevin raised both of his—and he sat down in his pajamas to eat.

After breakfast everyone scattered to do their last-minute chores. Kevin went into his bedroom to get dressed . . . but he didn't.

A few minutes later I called to Kevin, "Kevin, it's almost

time to leave for nursery school. You had better get dressed. I'm not going to tell you again."

"Okay," said Kevin, as he raced his car along the block road, over the bridge and made a screeching stop next to his block house. Then he noticed the house needed a roof and a garage and was still working on that task when Jan gave the final call, "Get into the car. It's time for school."

"But I'm not dressed!" said Kevin.

"That's too bad," I said. "You will just have to go to nursery school in your pajamas."

"But my friends will laugh at me!"

"Then get your clothes quickly. You will have to get dressed in the car. We are leaving right now!" I said as I headed for the door.

Kevin grabbed some clothes and raced for the car. It was a short ride to nursery school, so Kevin dressed quickly. Off came his pajamas; on went his underpants; on went the blue shirt. He buttoned it as fast as he could. When he finished there was one extra button at the top and one extra button-hole at the bottom.

Then he put on the old torn green pants and one brown sock. Where was the other sock? He searched the car. No sock. He must have dropped it. What should he do?

"Well," said Kim, trying to be helpful, "one sock is better than no socks."

It wasn't easy for me to let him go to school in that condition. He looked like a neglected child. But the lesson he learned was worth it.

When there is no natural consequence, or the natural consequence is harmful, parents must impose a consequence that will help the child see the folly of his behavior and learn a lesson from the experience. You can't allow a two year old to run out into the street. The natural consequence is that she might get killed. You can't allow a ten year old to pick your neighbor's apples without asking. The neighbor might verbally rip the child apart or send for the police. Or getting away with the theft might encourage this behavior in the future.

Instead, in such cases, you must teach a child what is inappropriate by using a parent-imposed logical consequence. For example, "If you can't stay out of the street you'll have to play in the fenced back yard." "If you pick our neighbor's apples, I will have to take $10 from your allowance, and together we will tell Mr. Johnson that this money is your payment for the apples."

Imposing a logical consequence can teach a child a lifetime lesson. Gordon never forgot the time his father took away his car. Dad had told him when he turned sixteen and got a car that he would lose the privilege of driving it if he disregarded certain guidelines, one of which was that he was not to drive out of town without asking first.

One day when Dad was doing business in a nearby town, he was surprised to see Gordon drive down the street with a car full of kids. When Gordon got home, Dad put Gordon's car in the garage, jacked it up, removed all four wheels, rolled them to the side of the garage and padlocked them together.

Needless to say, Gordon had quite a shock when he discovered it. His dad told him matter-of-factly why the wheels were locked up. Gordon couldn't have the key to unlock the wheels for a month, even though the prom was just two weeks away.

Gordon learned that when Dad said something he meant it. And as far as Dad knows, his son never again ignored a rule that carried consequences.

Some parents say, "I use parent-imposed consequences all the time. If my child breaks a window, I spank him. If he gets into a fight, I spank him. If he spills his milk, I spank him." These are parent-imposed consequences, but they are NOT logical consequences that are related to a child's specific behavior.

To be most effective, a parent-imposed consequence must be clearly linked to a child's behavior. If a child breaks a window, let her clean up the mess (if she is old enough not to get cut), apologize to the owner, and pay for the damages. If a child gets into a fight, a logical consequence might be, "If you can't get along, you two will have to be separated or sit in the talk-it-over chairs (two facing chairs) where children must sit until they have settled their dispute." Even a young child can wipe up spilled milk and learn a lesson about the consequences of carelessness.

The beauty of using natural and logical consequences is that a child can never truthfully shout "Unfair." He begins to learn that the discipline fits the act, and that he deserves to suffer the consequences.

If you're sold on the concept of making your child's "punishment" fit her "crime," then you'll want to make sure you follow these guidelines.

1. Don't shield your child from consequences that would be, in the long run, beneficial to him.

2. Don't allow your child to blame others for the predicament she got herself into. Neither should you cast blame on your child. It is enough that she is suffering from the consequences of her act.

3. If the natural consequence is too harmful, or if there is no immediate consequence, impose a logical consequence that is linked to his unacceptable behavior.

4. Support your child in accepting a consequence as a beneficial experience. Encourage her to keep a positive attitude about the experience. Help her develop the attitude that a valuable lesson can be learned from each mistake.

5. Don't let your child face a major or traumatic consequence without your support. Stay close to him, if possible, and let him know that you care. Otherwise, he may become discouraged, and discouragement leads to misbehavior.

6. Decide in advance what logical consequences you would impose on your child for the following acts:

Screaming and yelling when you have asked her to be quiet.

Breaking a toy through carelessness.
Eating a candy bar before lunch.
Playing with matches.
Scribbling on the wall.
Hammering dents in the table.
Telling a lie.
Being disrespectful to an adult.
Forgetting to notify you when he will be late.
Going someplace without permission.

Please stop right here unless you have already done as I suggested and thought of a logical consequence for each of the above. If you didn't, take a second look at the list. It's easier to think of a logical consequence for some kinds of misbehavior than for others, isn't it? For example, if your child screams after you say "Be quiet," you can remove him from your hearing. For breaking a toy—well, she has to do without or maybe pay to get it fixed. Eating a candy bar before lunch might mean no dessert. Matches aren't playthings and should be taken away and hidden. If he scribbles on the wall—he cleans the wall, and for hammering on the table, the hammer is taken away.

You may have to think for a while about an appropriate consequence for forgetting to notify you when he'll be late or going someplace without permission. Maybe losing the privilege of going someplace special might fit. A consequence for being disrespectful may be separation from the adult by being sent to a time-out room. But what consequence fits telling a lie? Here you may have to look for a consequence that is associated with the content of the lie. For example, if the child lies about raiding the cookie jar, maybe she shouldn't get a cookie the next time they are served for dessert. If the child says she didn't watch TV when she did, perhaps she shouldn't be allowed to watch TV for a while!

Just remember, although it's not always easy to think of a logical consequence, the closer the consequence is to fitting the crime, the more effective it is likely to be!

It doesn't take much experience for children to have a pretty good idea about what would be a fair consequence for their misbehavior. So, if you're in question about what to do, or if your child is older and you feel he may resent your discipline, treat him as God treated King David and allow the child to choose the consequences. God told David not to take a census of the people, but David wanted to know how great his kingdom was, so he went against God's instructions. To teach David the importance of obedience, God was going to impose a consequence, but He gave David the choice—three years of famine, three months of pursuit in battle, or three days of a fatal plague in the land (see 2 Sam 24).

For some reason, self-imposed consequences are always a little easier to bear. But they can teach a lesson nevertheless. After Kent had been caught whittling holes in his desk, the teacher asked that he talk to his parents about what should be done. Rather than face them, Kent lied to his teacher, saying he had talked to his parents and they were too busy to fix the desk. Later, his parents learned of the situation and after talking with Kent decided that, in addition to fixing the desk, the lesson of truthfulness should be emphasized. Kent was allowed to choose one of three consequences: not play games with the family that day, forfeit his night out with Dad, or work for two hours weeding the garden. He chose the two-hour weeding job.

Rather than risk the child's resentment of what he considers unjust discipline, allow him to choose even if you feel his choice may be too lenient. If the lesson is learned, the severity of the consequence doesn't matter. Most parents feel discipline has to be painful. If you make it unpleasant enough the child will never forget the lesson you wanted him to learn. That's not necessarily so. One mother told me a story about how a sugar cube taught her daughter a lesson that lasted a lifetime—and I think it's worth sharing.

Janine had been grumpy all day. Nothing had gone right. She complained about having to get up. She complained about having to set the table for breakfast. And, "Yucky, oatmeal again?"

Halfway through the morning Mom asked, "Janine, can you help me empty the wastebaskets?"

Janine, didn't budge. "I'm busy!" she said, not even looking up. Mom continued her cleaning and a few minutes later said, "Janine, I put all the wastebaskets in the hall. Please, can you empty them now so I can get the bedrooms finished?"

"I told you, I'm busy!" Janine responded in an irritated voice.

After lunch Mom asked Janine if she could clear the dishes away. Janine acted as if she'd been asked to move the Empire State Building. "I don't want to do it. It's too much work. I don't feel like working. This is my vacation. I shouldn't have to work."

And that's the way the day went until about 5 p.m. when Mom asked Janine if she could pick things up before Dad got home. At that simple request, Janine blew up. "Who was your slave last year? Work, work, work. All you do is nag—do this, do that—I can't stand it anymore." Janine turned around and stomped off to her room.

Mom knew that something had to be done, but what? What type of discipline could be strong enough to bring results? Mom gave Janine a few minutes to cool down and then knocked on her door. "Janine, may I come in?"

"Yes," Janine sighed. "Come in."

Mom whispered a prayer, took a deep breath and began her speech. "Janine, honey, we can't have this behavior anymore. You've been grumpy and negative all day. And you may not sass me! What do I need to do to teach you a lesson that you can't be so sour? I'll let you decide, but remember it must be something strong enough so that this will never happen again. What do you think I should do?"

Janine thought a few minutes and said, "Give me a sugar cube."

"A sugar cube?" That certainly wasn't what Mother had in

mind as discipline. "Why a sugar cube?"

"Because," said Janine, "I've been so sour, it will remind me to be sweet!"

"Are you sure it will work?" questioned a very doubtful mother.

"Yes, I'm sure," said Janine.

So Mom gave her a sugar cube—and it worked! Whenever Janine was tempted to be sassy and negative, Mom just asked her if she needed another sugar cube, and that's all it took to turn the sour to the sweet.

Isn't that what discipline's all about—teaching a lesson that will last a lifetime? If a sugar cube will do it, why not? Creative disciplinarians don't just haul off and hit a kid. They consider carefully the type of discipline that will teach the child the lifetime lesson that obedience pays. So, why not make your "punishment" fit the "crime," and start allowing your child to learn from the consequences!

CHAPTER 10

SAYING YES INSTEAD OF NO

If you want your children to be happy, cheerful, and have a positive outlook toward life, then you have to be a positive parent.

The YES method of child rearing should be your goal. It's much more effective than the NO method, but it doesn't come naturally. If you have ever said no to your child only to have her pout, kick or scream until you ended up saying yes, then you must have realized there has to be a better way. All you have to do the next time your child makes a request is to say yes first, unless you really mean no.

The following illustration shows how much more effective the YES method can be. Here's a typical fast-food restaurant scene:

Mom (to her preschooler): "Eat your burger."

Junior: "I wanna go play on the toys. Can I?"

Mom: "NO! Eat your lunch."

Junior (starting to pout): "But I wanna play."

Mom (getting frustrated): "I said eat your burger."

Junior (wiggling in his chair and faking a whimper): "I wanna play."

Mom has had it at this point and turns to her ten-year-old daughter across the table. "Shelly, take off your belt and hand it to me." Mom holds the belt in a threatening position while she glares at Junior, pouting in his chair. Slowly he reaches for his burger and takes a bite—and Mother turns back to the conversation she is having with a friend.

A few minutes later Junior notices the ice-cream cone his sister has gotten because she finished her meal, and he whines, "I wanna ice cream."

Mom ignores his request and blurts out, "Eat that burger at once or I'll use this belt."

Junior pouts quietly, then climbs out of his chair and rubs up against his mother. She reaches down and puts on his coat and tells sister, "Take him outside and watch him."

At last the little boy has gotten what he wanted, and he runs happily out to play on the inviting playground equipment. Later he comes back in to finish his meal and leaves with an ice-cream cone!

That's what happens far too often when parents say no. Kids have ways of either pouting or nagging their parents into giving in to them. If only this mother had used the YES method of child rearing, what a difference it would have made. For example, the scene could have gone like this:

Mom: "Eat your burger."

Junior: "I wanna go play on the toys. Can I?"

Mom: "Yes, you may go, just as soon as you take three more bites."

Junior then bites into the burger and runs happily off to play while Mom eats in peace. We might even pretend that the child runs back indoors and asks, "Mom, will you come and play?" And Mom, using the YES method might respond, "Yes, after I finish my burger. Do you want another bite?" And chances are the child will take a couple more bites before heading back out to the play equipment.

The YES method doesn't mean you're wishy-washy, and it doesn't mean you always allow your child to get her way. Everyone wins with the YES method. For example, going back to the restaurant scene, just look at the benefits of saying yes: Mother got to eat in peace; Junior got to play— and ended up eating just as much as he did with the threat of getting spanked. Sister got to play with a happy sib—and not baby-sit a pouting one. And everyone in the restaurant was able to enjoy their meal.

If the YES method sounds like something you need to cultivate, then start practicing the "yes-but" reply.

"Yes, I know you want to go, but have you considered how you will get your homework done?"

"Yes, you may play outdoors, but you must wear your long underwear, a heavy jacket, boots, earmuffs and only stay out 45 minutes."

"Yes, you can have Jill over to play, but you must get your practicing done first."

"Yes, you can go shopping for a new dress, but you'll have to earn the money to pay for it."

"Yes, you may watch the TV program, but you know our family policy about violence. At the first violent act you'll have to turn it off."

Children have the uncanny insight that enables them to recognize when their parents say no and don't really mean it. They then take advantage of this and pout or nag until they get their parents to change their minds. Does this sound familiar?

"Mother, can I have a stick of gum?"

"No."

"Why can't I have a stick of gum?"

"Because I said no."

"But I want a piece of gum."

"I told you you can't have a stick of gum."

"But I want a piece of gum. I want a stick of gum right now."

"I told you, you cannot have a stick of gum."

"Mommy, Jimmy has a stick of gum."

"I know. It doesn't matter if Jimmy has a stick of gum. I'm not going to give you a stick of gum."

"But Mommy, we've got sugarless gum. Why can't I have a stick of gum?"

"Because I told you, you can't have a stick of gum."

"Mommy, why can't I have a stick of gum?"

"Because I'm too busy. I have many things to do, and I'm not going to get up one more time just to get you a stick of gum."

"Mommy, what if I get it myself? Can I have a piece of gum?"

"Oh, okay, you can have a stick of gum. Get it yourself if you want it."

What has happened? The child has won. But the sad thing is that Mom not only let the child win—she rewarded him for nagging by saying what I call an "idiot no" in the beginning. An "idiot no" is an impulsive reaction; a no without much thought behind it. Children are quick to discern idiot no's, and they will persist until they find what will turn that idiot no into a yes.

It is a known fact that parents say no to their children's requests much more often than they say yes. Without thinking and for no good reason, the no just tumbles out!

So, for the creative parent, here's a good rule to follow: if you don't want your children pouting and nagging you into changing your mind, only say no when you are absolutely sure that you mean no and won't under any circumstances change your mind.

Get into the habit of saying "yes." The next time your child says, "Can I have dessert?" don't say no say, "Yes, just as soon as you finish your vegetables." When she says in the evening, "May I play outside?" say, "Yes, the first thing in the morning." When your teen wants to use the car, say, "Yes, but it needs to be washed first."

In other words, say "yes," unless you have a really good reason for saying no and will stick to your decision no matter what. You'll be surprised how often you can say yes to your child and how happy your positive response will make her feel. This was demonstrated to me one night when I was trying to put two-year-old Kevin to bed in his crib. "Mommy sleep with me?" he asked.

Immediately I said no. It seemed impossible. Me in a crib? "I can't," I explained. "I sleep in my own bed with Daddy."

"Please, Mommy, sleep with me," he begged. I continued with my idiot no.

"I'm sorry, Kevin. If I don't sleep with Daddy, he'll be lonesome." (As if Kevin wasn't going to feel lonesome having to sleep alone!)

And to this Kevin replied, "Mommy, you tell Daddy to find another mommy for him so you can sleep with me!"

Well, that was too much. Why not sleep with him for a while? After all, the crib was guaranteed to hold 500 pounds—and Kevin and I together didn't even come close to that! I threw away the idiot no position I had taken and said, "Yes, Kevin, I'll sleep with you for a while—if I don't break your bed!" He giggled as I kicked off my shoes and climbed in, hoping no one would catch me in his crib. Sure I felt foolish, but Kevin felt like a king!

He snuggled up and immediately his tense little body relaxed. I whispered a story to him about a little boy I once knew who acted very much like someone Kevin was well acquainted with. And before too long, he caught on and shouted, "That's me!"

Then after a hug, an Eskimo kiss (rubbing noses), and a butterfly kiss or two where I fluttered my eyelash against his cheek, I said good night and climbed out of his crib. Minutes later Kevin was in dreamland. I've always been glad I recognized my idiot no when I did and said yes to Kevin's request. It made him a very happy little boy.

Why not say yes to the YES method of child rearing and revolutionalize your parenting?

CHAPTER 11

THE TEN-TO-ONE RULE

Children need positive attention. Criticism, complaining and negative comments are discouraging and often result in more misbehavior. But encouragement, optimism and positive strokes are to kids as fertilizer is to plants. It's the stuff that really makes them flourish.

Rudolf Dreikurs, the highly respected child psychiatrist, once said, "Encouragement is more important than any other aspect of child raising. It is so important that the lack of it can be considered the basic cause for misbehavior. A misbehaving child is a discouraged child. Each child needs continuous encouragement just as a plant needs water. He cannot grow and develop and gain a sense of belonging without encouragement."

In my own child rearing I have found this to be true. For example, a number of years ago my husband, Jan, and I began noticing that the sunshine and laughter had disappeared from our little Kari. Her negative attitude was difficult to live with. She always seemed to be doing things that forced us to correct her. After realizing that our interactions with Kari were constantly critical, Jan decided to become her ally. I would continue to correct her when necessary, Jan would play the role of her advocate to support and encourage her, and we both would make a point of noticing and rewarding her good behavior.

Kari never knew anything about our plan, but within two

days she was dancing circles around her daddy. "Oh, Daddy, I love you so much." "Daddy, can we go out and get the wood together?" "Daddy, I want you to sit beside me." The little grouch had disappeared, and we were once more blessed with the warmth of her laughter.

What made the difference? Our criticism had discouraged her, and we ended up with a misbehaving child. Our encouragement and acceptance gave her a new sense of hope and enough ego strength to discipline herself into more appropriate behavior.

Behavior that gets your attention is rewarded and reinforced. Why not reward the positive? If you want to be a creative disciplinarian it's very important to catch your children being good. In fact, the ten-to-one rule is what I recommend: ten positive strokes to every negative one! Applying this rule will help you become the positive parent you've always wanted to be.

Marcia had always admired positive people. When she was in college she had the opportunity to spend a summer with a family who had two young children. For three months she never heard that mom and dad raise their voices to the children. And she determined that someday she wanted to be that kind of parent.

But nine years later, with four-year-old twin boys racing around the house, her dream of being a positive parent was pretty much shattered. She really hadn't realized just how negative she had become, however, until she decided to record an hour of her interactions with the children. Her purpose was to play the recording back so her boys could listen to it and discuss their negative behavior. But when she began to listen to the tape, the finger of guilt pointed to her. She heard herself saying: "Stop that." "Don't touch the stereo." "No, you can't have it now, I'm busy." "Bryan, if you do that again, you're going to get it." "Brent, no more sassing." "No." "Don't." "Stop!"

She couldn't believe how negative she had become. What

happened to her dream of being a positive parent? She knew children thrived on encouragement, words of appreciation, and positive strokes. Yet, during that hour she had recorded, she found herself delving out ten negatives to every positive. She immediately determined to turn herself around. Her new goal was to give ten positives for every negative and see what a difference it made in her children's behavior.

It wasn't an easy assignment. The first thing Marcia began to work on was making requests in a positive way rather than a negative one. Instead of "Don't stand on the table," she said, "Jump to the floor." Instead of "Don't touch the stereo," she said, "I was listening to the music on that station. Please try to find it again for me."

To her surprise her boys became more compliant. She began to realize that the don'ts that she had been giving her children never told them what to do. By making the request positive it gave the children guidelines—a direction in which to move.

The second thing she began to change was her response to her children's requests. No matter what they seemed to ask, she found herself without thinking saying no. Now she began a more positive approach. When they asked for a cookie between meals, instead of saying no, she would say, "Cookies are for dessert. I have saved this special one for you." If they wanted to watch TV and nothing appropriate was on, she would say, "Let's get the TV schedule and figure out a time when a program is on that you would like to watch." Then she would put forth extra effort to get the boys involved with another activity to take their minds off the TV.

Of course, like any normal person, Marcia found it impossible to be positive all the time. There were still times when a firm no needed to be said. Inappropriate behavior had to be corrected. And occasionally, when she was tired and frustrated, she found herself handing out negative strokes in the form of criticism and threats. But when this happened, she renewed her determination to use the ten-to-one rule. Ten positive strokes for every negative one.

Applying the ten-to-one rule meant that every time Marcia handed out a negative stroke she had to really look for the positives. She began to notice the little things the boys did that she approved of, and she let them know in the form of a compliment or just a hug or a wink.

It didn't take long for this positive treatment to have an effect on the family. The boys seemed happier. Instead of being bent on persecuting her, they were eager to please. Life was not always a bed of roses, but it was a lot more fun than it had been in the past.

The lack of positive attention can cause tremendous behavior problems in children. For example, one mother complained, "I'm having real problems with my five-year-old son, Kurt. He is sassy and willful. Whatever I ask him to do, he does the opposite. I can't understand this since his older brother, Dean, is such a jewel. I try to treat them the same but I find myself spending more time with Dean because he is such a pleasant person. Why is there such a difference in their behavior?"

It's really surprising, isn't it, when one child is so good and the next so "bad"? Even though you treat both of them the same, you seem to get opposite results. The reason for this is that children are born with different characteristics which may either make them easy or difficult to live with. But regardless of their inborn characteristics, all children need positive attention. They need to feel special. They need to hear compliments and receive recognition.

When one child in the family is supercompliant and naturally receives abundant amounts of positive attention, the more difficult child notices, at least on an unconscious level. It's interesting how often it is the firstborn who seems to go along with what the parents say, and the second who rebels. The younger begins to feel that the older child (or the submissive child) has a monopoly on getting attention for compliance. The second child reasons that he could not possibly be as good, no matter how hard he tries, so why compete?

But the difficult child needs and craves attention, so he chooses another area in which to excel—often opting for the role of the rebel. He would rather have negative attention than little or no attention at all.

Chances are this need for attention was what was causing Kurt to be so obnoxious. The question is, how can you modify the behavior of a child like Kurt? Here are some ideas:

1. Make sure both children have their share of positive recognition. This may mean noticing a lot more of the positive things that Kurt does; things that to you may seem insignificant. Reward him for little bits of compliance.

2. Make it fun and easy for Kurt to obey. For a while, don't ask him to do things when you know he will resist. You want as much compliance as possible so you can give more positive attention.

3. Be firm on the limits that are absolutely essential. Don't accept disrespectful or sassy behavior—but don't give him a lot of negative attention for this either. When it happens, calmly say, "I feel hurt when you treat me like that, and you may not hurt others." And then you can send him to his room until he chooses to act appropriately, or impose some other type of discipline.

4. Finally, follow the ten-to-one rule that Marcia decided to follow. Try to give your child ten positive strokes to every negative one. Because the more difficult child is obviously going to get a few more negative strokes, you must proportionally increase the positive interactions with him in order for it to have the same effect. For example, you might notice Kurt's smile, his remembering to say please and thank you, or just his willingness to spend a few extra minutes playing with the dog who doesn't get much attention. You've got to become a master at catching your child being good.

Remember, a positive stroke doesn't always have to be given in words. Smile, wink, ruffle his hair—and he will get the message that you're tuned in to him and you will be filling his love cup. It can be quite a challenge but it is worth it.

If you think your children deserve a more positive parent and could use more of your positive attention, why don't you do what Marcia did—and what Kurt's mom decided to do. Record an hour or so of your interactions with your children. If you are leaning toward the negative, I would challenge you to apply the ten-to-one rule in your family. Ten positives to every negative. And I will guarantee that your children will blossom under this positive "rule" and you'll all enjoy life together a whole lot more!

CHAPTER 12

ESTABLISHING VALUES EARLY

Many of the behaviors you like or dislike in your child directly reflect what you value. For example, there's really nothing wrong with your child's eating with her fingers, if her fingers are clean. Whether a child should use fingers or a fork is dictated by values. How important is it to you that your children abide by culturally accepted norms? Other areas of behavior that reflect values might include the following:

1. Religious behavior such as saying the blessing before eating or not misusing the name of God.

2. Social behavior such as standing when you are introduced to a person who is standing or not interrupting adults who are talking.

3. Recreational activities. Going to movies or listening to rock music may be right or wrong depending upon your values. Other parents object to recreational hunting or playing with war toys.

4. Health behavior, such as going to sleep at a regular time, avoiding junk foods, and not eating between meals may reflect individual values.

5. Acceptable appearance has to do with values. Some parents insist that their children wear suits and ties to church. Others disprove of new hairstyles or false eyelashes. Some have a hang-up about wearing stripes and plaids together!

6. Behavior and attitudes about school may also reflect values. It's not morally wrong to get C's or D's in school nor

will low grades always hurt a child, but the way some parents react, you would think it was the end of the world!

The majority of corrections that parents impose on their children are a direct reflection of their own values. These are behaviors the parent feels strongly about, not because these behaviors hurt the individual, others or things, but because it's something they value personally.

Parental values differ. You and your spouse may not agree on such things as the importance of maintaining a vegetarian diet, the significance of getting to bed at a decent hour, or how much time a child needs for free play. These value clashes can cause major conflicts, leaving the child uncertain about what is really important.

It's also true that certain behavior may be tolerated in one household and strictly forbidden in another. Since there is nothing inherently right or wrong in these behaviors, it can lead to severe parent-child conflicts because the child can't understand why her friend gets away with behavior that is strictly forbidden for her.

The way to minimize these conflicts as much as possible is to clearly establish what is acceptable value-related behavior and to do it as early in life as possible—preferably during infancy. Then when you hear, "But Jimmy gets to do that. Why can't I?" you have an answer. If you have clearly established acceptable behavior for your family, you can say, "This is something that the Kuzma family feels is important." Or "Our family's values are different and we couldn't allow that." You may also say, "Because I feel so strongly about that, I can't let you do it—it would hurt me if you did." When a value clash occurs with older children who will make their own decisions regardless of your values, you may have to say, "What you want to do conflicts with my value system. But you are now old enough to establish your own values." Then after explaining the reason you value what you do, you might say, "I hope you will carefully consider why I value what I do before making your decision."

One of the best ways for young children to "catch" your values is to let them hear you expressing them within their hearing, but not directed toward them. Often a conversation overheard will have more impact than words spoken specifically to them.

The chances are slim that your children will grow up with exactly the same values as you. They may be similar, but even slight differences in the area of values can cause conflict. A wise parent must understand this and not force her own values on the child. Only two options remain: to teach by precept and to teach by example. To teach by precept (instruction) means to admonish or to influence your child from an early age according to a basic standard of conduct. In addition you should present information and encourage unemotional discussions about the rationale behind your values. To teach by example you must be consistently living by your values. You cannot have one set of values that you try to impose on your children while you live by another.

When Lily's daughter, Maria, was just six she became enthralled by the gaudy jewelry, excessive makeup and long, painted artificial fingernails that she observed on others. TV added fuel to the fire of her desire to "look beautiful." The problem was that Lily's value system was very different. She believed in a simple, modest, unpretentious look. She believed in natural beauty—being physically fit, having healthy skin, wearing only a little makeup and almost no jewelry. Of course, she wanted Maria to feel the same way. Lily was really worried. If Maria had such a strong desire for artificial "beauty" at age six, what would she be like at sixteen with the weird hairstyles and immodest fashions that might well be in vogue?

Wisely Lily recognized that strictly to forbid certain things might make them more enticing to her youngster, until obtaining the forbidden becomes the burning desire. She certainly didn't want that. Lily hoped that once Maria's curiosity was satisfied it would be a passing fancy.

Lily approached the issue by saying, "It's fun to look pretty. God loves beauty, too. That's why He made us just the way we are. But God says that what is on the inside is really the most important. He wants you to have a beautiful personality; to be friendly and kind.

"Sometimes people think they can get more attention by putting on gaudy jewelry and wearing brightly colored make-up and long, artificial fingernails. I don't think this is necessary. I believe in modesty and simplicity. But if you would like to dress up and pretend you are a fancy lady, like the ones you see on TV, then I'll help you. But when you go outside our home, to school or to church, I want people to see God's beautiful creation—the real you—and not just man-made jewelry and colored paint on your face and nails. Okay?" (Lily also didn't want Maria to be rewarded by having others give her a lot of attention when wearing these things.)

Well, that has worked with Maria—at least for now. If the issue surfaces again, Lily might have to say, "Maria, there are many people you can look to in this world as an example of what is an appropriate appearance. I would be happy if you'd follow my example. You can wear as much makeup, colored nail polish and jewelry as I wear. Or you might enjoy taking a beauty and poise class where you can learn to apply makeup and accessories in such a way as to enhance your God-given beauty and not detract from it. Plus, I believe that wearing the proper colors that compliment your skin tones and having the right hairstyle for your face has much more to do with being attractive than wearing excessive makeup and jewelry. Would you like to have a professional help you in these areas?"

This approach may resolve the value conflict—at least for a while. But what should Lily do when Maria is sixteen and insists she wants to wear a wild hairstyle or short skirts and see-through blouses?

The answer depends on the strength of Lily's values. Some mothers might feel that by sixteen years of age a girl should be able to make choices about her personal appearance. Others would take a stronger stand. "No, I'm sorry, I cannot let you wear immodest styles or styles that represent values very different from our own. Our family believes in simplicity and modesty—and one way we have lived that value is in appearance. This is so important to me, that I must take a strong stand and say no. I hope you will understand."

But what if she doesn't? What if this continues to be an issue? The resolution of this value conflict will be determined by four things: One, how firmly Lily has established the foundation for this value in early childhood—through both precept and example. Two, the reasonableness of the value. Does it make sense? Three, the quality of the rapport between parent and child. And four, the influence of significant peers.

If Maria loves her mother and doesn't want to hurt her, this will influence her decision regardless of peer pressure. But if Maria is rebelling and doesn't care about her mother's feelings, or if she wants to intentionally hurt her mother, then watch out!

You cannot dictate what values your children will ultimately hold. But if you want them to respect your values and if you want to increase the chances of their living by them during their growing years, then in addition to maintaining a good relationship with your children, be sure your values are reasonable, that you establish them early, and that you consistently maintain them through instruction and example.

CHAPTER 13

IS THE PROBLEM WITH THE CHILD OR THE SITUATION?

Many parents believe that if they are wise enough, smart enough, and skilled enough, they can pretty well solve their child's behavior problems. That's not really true. No matter how many strategies you may use, some problems are beyond your control.

Why? Because there are two kinds of problems kids have: situation problems that can be solved by modifying the situation or environment in some way, and person problems that can be solved only when the person with the problem chooses to change.

Most early behavior problems are situation problems. These are problems that can be solved by a situational change. You can ward off the problem by meeting your child's needs before he has to misbehave to get your attention. In other cases, you take control and through discipline the problem is solved. Here are some common situation problems and their solutions.

Your baby cries: You change the diaper. The crying stops.

Your toddler throws food from the table: Her plate is removed and no more throwing.

Your child is whining: You put the child in bed for a nap and then he wakes up happy.

Your kids are throwing their jackets on the floor: You provide a coatrack right by the front door, and they begin hanging up their jackets.

IS THE PROBLEM WITH THE CHILD OR THE SITUATION?

Joyce experienced a typical situation problem with four-year-old Betsy. Betsy was making everyone late for school. After breakfast, instead of brushing her teeth and putting on her coat so she was ready to leave, she just dawdled. Mom tried getting her up earlier in the morning, but that didn't seem to help. Even when breakfast was over ahead of schedule, Betsy still couldn't get ready on time.

Finally Mom talked to Betsy about the problem and learned that even though Betsy loved kindergarten, she really wanted to spend more time with her mom. By dawdling each morning she was able to get more of her mom's attention, even though it was mostly negative.

Joyce admitted that the morning hours were hectic, and Betsy didn't get much attention unless she misbehaved. So she decided to try an experiment. She made lunches and set the table the night before so she would have an extra twenty minutes in the morning to devote to Betsy. She would read to her, play dolls, or have a tea party—whatever Betsy wanted. The result? Betsy blossomed with this extra attention and the problem disappeared.

Joyce realized that the problem of not getting ready for school on time was not Betsy's problem per se, but a situational problem brought on by Betsy's need for attention. Joyce's plan of attack, therefore, was to change the situation, and the problem was quickly resolved. If Joyce had misdiagnosed the problem she would probably have doubled her efforts at correcting and criticizing Betsy and would have unknowingly contributed to the problem.

Not all problems are as simple to solve. Sometimes you must change your plan of attack, or you must try a wide variety of solutions before you find one that really works. Often, situation problems that could have been easily solved by a change in the environment become deep-seated person problems that affect every aspect of a child's life for many years to come—such as getting into the habit of showing off in order to get attention, or lying out of fear of harsh punishment. This is behavior you want to prevent.

Some problems are a combination of the two. They may start out as a situation problem, but fairly quickly move into the arena of a person problem. This is especially true when problems become habits. For example, have you ever tried to cure a five-year-old thumb sucker? You remind her 386 times a day, put yucky tasting stuff all over her thumbs, make her wear mittens to bed and pay the dentist to install an antithumb sucking device in her mouth. But after all your well-meaning effort, your five year old is still sucking away. Why? Because the problem has become a person problem and is no longer a situation problem.

At birth, thumb sucking might be considered a situation problem. If parents are consistent and persistent enough the child will often accept a pacifier. If not, thumb sucking quickly becomes a habit—a person problem. And when this happens the only way the parent-imposed situational reminders can help is if the child wants to stop sucking her thumb.

The longer inappropriate actions are tolerated, the more they become a part of the child's spontaneous behavior. Once this occurs, then no amount of parental pressure, manipulation, strategy, or punishment will work. Change will come only after the child chooses to change. It's at this time (when a child wants to change) that a motivational reminder may be most helpful. At least that's what it took to solve Henry's teasing problem.

Henry was a saint with other people, but when he got around his younger brothers and sisters, his halo disappeared. He teased them unmercifully. No matter what they said, he would retort with some "catty" remark. He made everyone in the family miserable. He was no fun to be around.

Mom was beside herself. There must be some way to get Henry to change his snide remarks into kind ones. When Henry was younger she tried punishing him—sending him to the time-out room every time he teased.

When this didn't work, she made him say three nice things

about the person for every awful thing he said. But the tug-of-war that took place to extract words of kindness and appreciation from Henry was hardly worth it.

Mom tried withholding privileges. Once Henry went without his bike for a month; but no problem, he just took up skateboarding!

As Henry got older, he realized that teasing hurt people's feelings and it wasn't something he wanted to do, but still he couldn't seem to break his teasing habit.

It was then that Mom realized that Henry's problem was indeed Henry's problem. He admitted he wanted to change but couldn't. That's when they came up with the idea of a motivational reminder!

Without telling Henry, Mom purchased the baseball mitt Henry had been wanting, had it wrapped in a beautiful box and tied with a bow. She then took the box home to Henry and told him that there was something in the box that he really wanted, but the only way he could earn the right to open the package was to convince the family that teasing was no longer a part of his behavior.

Mom placed the package on top of the refrigerator where Henry would be sure to see it every time he walked by.

Henry slipped up a few times, but when he remembered the package he stopped himself. And his siblings were helpful, too. When he would begin to tease, all they had to say was, "Henry, remember the package!" and he would apologize.

The last time I talked to Henry's mom, the package had been sitting on the refrigerator for two months! But Henry had made definite improvement, and she was quite hopeful that the family would soon vote to allow Henry to open the package.

Why did the wrapped package work? Henry already knew he should change and he wanted to, but motivation was lacking. Seeing the package on top of the refrigerator every day made him want to change as soon as possible. So, if you have tried a dozen ways to get your child to stop a negative behavior and nothing works, admit defeat and try this approach:

1. Talk to your child about her problem. Help her to recognize it as her problem and point out the negative effect this behavior will have on her unless it is corrected.

2. Tell your child you are willing to help—but only if he wants to change and seeks your help. It just may be that a motivational reminder is all your child needs to give him the "ummph" to overcome that troublesome habit.

3. Start building your child's self-worth. Fill her love cup. Encourage. Instead of discipline, a completely different approach is now needed. Only people with a healthy dose of self-worth have the courage necessary to admit their errors and the ego strength necessary to harness the means to overcome their problems.

Remember, you cannot make your children perfect. Don't feel guilty or embarrassed over behavior you can't control. You do them an injustice if you accept the blame for problems that are really theirs. Help your children instead to see that they are the builders of their own personalities and reputations. They can choose the characteristics they want to develop. Sometimes they may feel like the apostle Paul and end up doing what they don't want to do and not doing what they know they should do. But Christ can give them the courage and the self-control necessary to change—if they ask for His help.

So if your child has a person problem and wants to solve it, encourage him or her to hold fast to the promise in Mark 10:27, "all things are possible with God."

CHAPTER 14

RAISING RESPONSIBLE CHILDREN

Do you sometimes feel like a nagging ninny standing over your kids telling them every move to make? "Brush your teeth; make your bed; empty the trash." You hate to be so bossy, but what else can you do when kids don't do what they're supposed to?

Nagging will never turn irresponsible children into responsible ones, but I know four powerful strategies that will. The first has to do with encouraging your child to be his own boss, and the second is to challenge him to retrain you—his bossy parent! The third has to do with teaching your child to be a good decision maker so you won't need to tell him what to do. And the fourth is to trade a privilege for a responsibility. Here's how these strategies work.

Bossing can become an irritating way of life—a trap that older, more capable family members fall into. I know. It's happened to us. When Kevin was younger, Mom, Dad and two big sisters all told him what to do—over and over. But it wasn't until six-year-old cousin Jennifer asked, "Why does everyone boss Kevin around?" that we recognized how bossy we had become. I decided I'd have to do something to encourage Kevin to take responsibility for his own behavior. So, one night as I was tucking him into bed I asked, "Kevin, do you like getting bossed around?"

"No," he said emphatically.

"Then you've got to be your own boss. Nobody will boss

you around if you take control of your own life. When you do what you're supposed to do, nobody has to nag you. So whose fault is it that you get bossed?"

"Mine, I guess," he said sheepishly.

"That's right. Either you be your own boss and tell yourself what to do, or somebody else will have to boss you."

"But it's hard," sighed Kevin. "I don't like to do all the things I have to do."

"The things still have to be done. So either you take control of your life—or we'll boss you around. What will it take to get your boss to work?"

"Well, Mom, remember that little truck with the motorcycles in the back?"

"Okay, that will be your boss's salary for two full days of work. I'll help you make a list each morning. You have until noon to prove that your boss is working. No one will remind or nag. But at noon, if your boss is not doing his job, then the rest of the family has the right to begin bossing you around— and that day won't count toward your truck. Remember, it has to be two full days in a row! Do you think your boss is strong enough to handle you?"

"I think so."

I leaned over and kissed his forehead. "Your boss will need a lot of rest. He'll be taking over the job of four people. Instead of everybody else bossing you around, he'll have to do it all by himself. Good night, Boss," I whispered as I closed the door.

Well, two days later Kevin's boss had earned his salary— the truck with the motorcycles in the back. The biggest problem was retraining Kevin's four previous bosses! But with Kevin taking responsibility for his own life, we soon settled back into our proper roles of controlling ours.

Getting your child to take responsibility for her own behavior by becoming her own boss is an especially helpful technique for young children. But as children get older I've discovered an even more effective strategy.

There are many kids who resent how their parents treat them, and they blame their parents. What they don't realize is that their parents are probably treating them exactly the way irresponsible children deserve to be treated. But if you say that straight out kids won't buy it. So, I enjoy challenging kids with the fact that they have the power to change their parents. It may be hard to "teach an old dog new tricks," but it is possible. And it's the same with parents. They're not easy to retrain. But sometimes it's important to try. Here's how strategy number two works.

I once met a teenager who complained bitterly about the way his father treated him. "Dad never says he loves me or asks how my day went, he just constantly tells me things to do. Whenever he sees me, he says something like, 'Jack, help your mother set the table,' or 'Jack, have you fed the dog yet?' I'm so sick of it, I try to hide when he comes home and avoid him as much as I can."

"Wow," I replied. "You've got a real problem, don't you?"

"I sure do," he mumbled. "Why does he have to pick on me? He never says those things to my sisters. They can be sitting in the same room—but it's always me he tells to do something."

As I listened I began to put the pieces together. Jack's sisters were always busy. They had certain responsibilities which they carried out without being asked, and when they weren't busy with their chores, they were either practicing their musical instruments or doing their homework.

Jack, on the other hand, shirked responsibility. He hated to do chores so he always waited until his dad got on his case before he did what he needed to do. Jack admitted that he didn't like to practice, so he put it off as long as possible. Play came first, and homework was only tackled when he was threatened or forced. So, by shirking responsibilities, Jack had trained his dad to tell him what to do—and a negative pattern of interaction had developed.

"Well," I said to Jack, "It seems to me you've got a big job ahead. You've trained your dad to treat you like this—and now you've got to retrain him to treat you the way you want to be treated."

"Yeah, I sure wish I could. But Dad will never change."

"Hey, don't say that. He's not like that to your sisters, so it seems to me it's your problem. And it's your responsibility to retrain him."

"How do I do that?"

"Simple," I said. "You figure out what your dad wants you to do, and do it before he has a chance to tell you. If you know he wants you to feed the dog before he gets home from work, then do it. When he gets home and says, 'Jack, feed the dog,' all you have to say is, 'I already did it.' After a week or two of you saying, 'I already did it,' chances are he won't feel he needs to remind you anymore—so he won't."

"But what if I don't want to feed the dog?"

"Well, if it's your responsibility, and you don't want to do it, then I guess you'll just have to put up with your dad bugging you. It's all up to you. Tell you what, Jack. Why don't you try it for a week? Do everything you should do before your dad has a chance to tell you—and see if it doesn't make a difference in the way he treats you. I think your dad's a pretty smart guy. I have a feeling he can be retrained."

Well, Jack took me up on my challenge and is enjoying a new relationship with his dad. It was worth the extra effort it took to retrain his dad.

If you've got a child suffering from this same problem—having to live with a parent who needs "retraining," why don't you try this strategy on her—and challenge her to see if she can't retrain you. Parents can learn new tricks!

Children become good decision makers by making decisions. But just how early can you give them this responsibility? When can you trust your child to make good decisions? Try the SEA decision-making strategy and find out.

At a very early age, your child can learn to make simple decisions. He should be making his own decisions if he can

Seek the information he needs to make a good decision; *Evaluate* the alternatives without bias; and *Accept* the consequences of his decision. The acronym to remember is SEA. S for seeking information; E for evaluating the alternatives, and A for accepting the consequences.

Here is how this strategy works. Let's say your three year old wants to run out into a busy street. You don't allow her to make such a decision. She is too young to understand or seek the crucial information about the speed and momentum of moving vehicles relative to three-year-old legs. Evaluating the pros and cons of running into the street is beyond her ability, and the consequences are too severe. So you impose your own decision.

But the same three year old may be ready to make a simple, nonthreatening choice, such as whether or not to eat between meals. My daughter, Kim, made this choice when she was three. She wanted a cookie. I said no. She insisted. She nagged. So I put the SEA strategy to a test.

I gave her information on why I disapproved of her eating cookies between meals. When her tummy was filled with a sugary cookie, it wouldn't be hungry for the healthy food that we'd be having for supper. The alternatives I gave her were simple: have one cookie now and nothing for supper, or two cookies as dessert after supper. The consequences of eating a cookie before supper were not life threatening. Yes, she might not be hungry for supper, and it could even lead to a habit (which she'd have to overcome later) of snitching junk food between meals, but none of the consequences were great enough for me to feel that she wasn't capable of making the decision. So, after I was sure she understood the consequences, I allowed her to decide.

No more nagging. She decided it would be better to wait until supper.

I can't promise that your child will make a similar decision. At the time, I was unsure about Kim. I had no way of knowing what she would do. And I'm smart enough to know that just because it works once doesn't mean it will continue to work. But a child needs to be given the opportunity to learn how to struggle with decision making. Indispensable to learning is the need to make poor decisions and suffer the consequences!

Some children pick up the SEA strategy quickly and become mature decision makers at a surprisingly early age. You may have a precocious child. But, you will never know until you take the risk yourself and put SEA to the test.

One of the biggest areas of conflict between parents and older children is over decision making. Children need to become independent and learn to make good decisions on their own, but when it comes to major decisions, too many parents take over.

Just how far would you go in allowing your child to make decisions on his own? Would you allow him to decide such things as whether or not he needed a curfew time? With the SEA strategy you should be fairly safe. But you have to make sure your children can get all the information they need, will not be biased as they consider the alternatives, and will not suffer consequences that are too severe. Sometimes it might take a little creativity to make sure that they can get all the information—including the possible consequences. Here's what happened to one family who decided to trust their children's decision-making abilities.

During the children's early years, Mom and Dad made most of the major decisions for the family. But now that the kids were in their teens the parents felt that the children should have a say. So it was decided that family policy would be discussed at a family council and then voted on. The majority would win. Now this took a lot of parental faith in the decision-making ability of their three children—because the parents could get outvoted.

At one family council meeting, the parents brought up the issue of having a curfew time. They knew that if they gave their children enough information and the reasons why a curfew was important, they'd vote for a reasonable curfew. The matter was discussed at length, and Dad called for the vote. Three to two, the children outvoted their parents. No curfew.

Mom was beside herself. Enough of this democratic stuff. "I can't live not knowing where the kids are or what time they will return."

"Just a minute," said Dad. "The children just don't have enough information yet." And then Mom and Dad sat down and planned a way for the children to get the information they needed to make a good decision.

The next afternoon, without telling the children, Mom packed her suitcase and left the house, planning to spend the night with friends. About suppertime the kids began to ask, "Where's Mom? We're starved."

"Well," said Dad, "since your mom isn't home, you kids better get something to eat."

Throughout the evening hours, they kept wondering where Mom could be, but they really became worried about 10:30 p.m.

"Dad, where could Mom be? Even K-Mart's closed!"

"She's a big girl," replied Dad. "I think she can take care of herself. Go on to bed and don't worry."

Early the next morning the children rushed into their parents' bedroom and found only Dad. "Mom still isn't here? Where could she be?"

"I was just wondering that myself," said Dad.

Just as three frantic teenagers were rushing to the phone to report a missing mom, in she walked, suitcase in hand.

"Mom, where have you been?" they shouted. "And why didn't you come home last night?"

"Why?" she replied. "I thought we voted we didn't have to tell anyone where we were going or what time we would return."

"But Mom, you're a MOTHER!" And then light began to dawn. Immediately they called a family council and voted five to zero for a curfew. They wanted to know where their mother was going and what time she'd return.

It's true, children CAN make good decisions on their own—if they have enough information. I take my hat off to these creative parents who, instead of forcing an issue and then perhaps having to deal with three defiant teenagers, figured out a way to help their children gain the information they needed to make a responsible decision.

Children develop at their own individual rates. Some exhibit responsibility at an early age. Others are slow maturers. To grant privileges to all at a specific age is a risky idea. What if the child isn't ready to handle a privilege in a responsible manner? And yet children want privileges!

The answer is to trade a privilege for a responsibility. For example:

- You may drive the family car when you can pay for your own insurance.
- You may date when you can keep your room clean without being told to or getting paid for it.
- You may choose the number of hours you watch TV per week when you can maintain an acceptable grade average.

Mark resented his parents telling him it was bedtime. Now that he was twelve he figured he was old enough to make that decision for himself. Dad disagreed. He knew that if Mark stayed up too late, he was grouchy the next morning, resisted getting up, and was late to breakfast. It was finally decided that Mark could choose his own bedtime as long as it was before 9:30 p.m., and as long as he got up happily with his own alarm and was ready for breakfast without a reminder. It worked!

When parents match a privilege with a responsibility, the child learns a valuable lesson of life—freedom comes with responsibility. In other words, the more responsible the child—the more privileges. It is a sad and frustrated adult who hasn't realized that freedom of choice brings a responsibility with it.

Trade a privilege for a responsibility and chances are, if the child wants the privilege badly enough—he'll stretch himself to be the responsible person that you want him to become.

The way you raise a responsible child is to get out of the driver's seat, so to speak, and let her take over the wheel. If you continue to stay in charge by constantly nagging, reminding, and making decisions for your child, she'll let you take over her responsibility, hoping someday you'll forget to remind her, and then if something doesn't get done, it's your fault for not reminding her.

Put the responsibility on her shoulders by using one of the above strategies. Then clearly spell out the consequences of what will happen if she fails to carry out her responsibility. As children get older, they can even help to determine what would be appropriate consequences. And if she fails, let her suffer the consequences. It may sound cruel—but it can be a powerful lesson!

Let your child know that there are many ways that people help themselves to remember what they need to do. One is to make a list. Another is to group tasks around a certain part of the day, such as "things to do before breakfast." Certain tasks can become habitual when you get in a good routine. If nothing else works, encourage your child to simply ask someone, "Is there anything else I need to do now?" If your child can't remember, there's a good chance someone else can.

Sometimes kids unconsciously neglect certain tasks because they hate them. Check with your child. If that's his problem, you can almost always come up with a compromise. Trade one of your tasks for one of his. Or work together—but let your child be responsible for asking you to work with him if he in turn helps you. Raising a responsible child is not always easy. Some kids, especially firstborns, seem to accept responsibility more readily. But some, unless you make a concerted effort and have a well-thought-out training program, will continue to resist taking responsibilities. And when their irresponsibility stretches into adulthood, they become a burden to all—even themselves!

Don't let this happen to your child. Start now to encourage the acceptance of responsibilities by using the Being Your Own Boss Strategy, the Retraining Your Parent Strategy, and the SEA Method of Decision Making and Trading a Privilege for a Responsibility. They work.

PART TWO

THE EMOTIONAL ATMOSPHERE AT HOME

CHAPTER 15

ARE YOU A CHILD ABUSER?

Y ou can never be effective in using creative discipline if you punish in anger or resort to abusive behavior to make your child obey. Creative discipline and abuse just don't mix.

Are you a child abuser? Before you impulsively say, "Why, of course not" please read on. This chapter is for EVERY parent because every parent is a potential child abuser.

I hate to admit it, but even with all my degrees in child development I have occasionally been abusive. I'll never forget one afternoon when I let my emotions get completely out of control. I had a thousand things to do, and nothing seemed to be going right. The house was in a shambles, and my three preschoolers were running around like a pack of hyenas. The louder they shrieked and hollered, the tighter my nerves wound.

To help me out of my mess, I had asked a teenager to come over and assist me in cleaning the house. Then I turned to my girls, "Kids, Molly is going to be vacuuming your bedroom soon. Please pick up the clothes that are on the floor."

They appeared to have heard me. But like so many parental commands, the words went in one ear and out the other. The clothes remained on the floor. However, this small fact didn't stop Molly from doing her job. She began vacuuming her way around the fallen garments. She had not been told to pick them up, so she left them on the floor. She had not counted on the strong suction of the vacuum, however, and before she knew it she had vacuumed up a beautiful, lace-trimmed nylon nightie.

The motor ground to a stop as the nightgown twisted around the brush and lodged in the vacuum's internal organs. The intense heat melted the nylon, leaving gobs of rock-hard bonding material on the metal parts of the vacuum.

This was the last straw. I couldn't believe the mess. What really upset me was how a teenager could be so dense as to not pick up the children's clothing before vacuuming. Yet I couldn't tell her that. Instead I vented my pent-up frustrations on my girls. I screamed, "Girls, look what you have done now. Why didn't you pick up your clothes? If you had only listened to me with half an ear, this would have never happened."

I began to cry as I started to disassemble the vacuum and realized the magnitude of the mess. "Just look at this mess. Your expensive nightgown is ruined, and this black nylon junk is stuck all over. It will probably cost a fortune to get this vacuum fixed. How could you have been so stupid!?"

I verbally ripped those kids up one side and down the other, never saying a thing to the teenager who was the immediate cause of the problem. The girls tried to tell me it was not their fault, but I would not listen. Finally, beaten down with verbal abuse, they retreated.

Left alone, scraping off the nylon globs, I began to think about the terrible way I had treated them. I knew better. I had written articles about verbal abuse and how careful we should be not to harm our children with demeaning words. I knew that such careless words could wound a child's sense of self-worth. I had even called such abuse psychological murder. And now I was guilty!

After I took the teenager home, I realized I had to apologize to my children. I called the girls to me, sat them on my lap and said how sorry I was for the way I had acted and the terrible things I had said.

Of course they forgave me. But I needed to do one more thing. I needed to make sure this didn't happen again. So, I gave my children permission to stop me if I ever verbally abused them again. I told them to say to me, "Mommy, you are out of control, and you told me to stop you."

Most of us think of child abuse as the harsh, irrational and violent treatment that leaves children physically injured and scarred for life. Child abuse conjures up in our minds bizarre pictures of children with black eyes and broken bones, first-degree burns from cigarettes or scalding water, whiplashing scars across the back and buttocks, or brain damage from having their heads battered against the wall.

This type of child abuse is a hideous crime. And most parents couldn't imagine ever treating a child in such a way. But there are milder types of child abuse that, chances are, we're all guilty of. The startling fact is that if your own child is over two years of age, child abuse has probably occurred in your own home, with you as the abuser and your child as the victim.

Child abuse is more than treatment that results in a physically battered child. It is any treatment that destroys the child's sense of personhood, his feelings of self-worth. It is the physical or verbal mistreatment of the child. Abusive behavior doesn't have to leave visible scars. It can leave internal scars—the kind that over time leave their mark on the child's thinking and personality. These are the scars that destroy self-worth.

If you accept this broad definition of child abuse then the following behaviors could be considered abusive.

1. Any physical punishment that the child feels is unjust or unreasonable—even though it may result in changed behavior.

2. Any impulsive, irrational punishment that is inflicted merely as an appeasement for parental anger.

3. Any treatment of the child that makes him feel embarrassed or belittled, especially when it occurs in public.

4. Any words that cut down her self-respect or diminish the positive feelings she has about herself.

5. Any behavior that causes the child to feel alienated from his family or God.

By now the finger of guilt is probably pointing in your direction. But guilt isn't going to help. What is needed is the firm resolve to discontinue these abusive actions—discontinue destructive punishment that only builds resentment and rebellion in the heart of your child.

Don't do what comes naturally. Don't base your discipline on how you were treated as a child. Nor should your discipline be based on present feelings. Rather, it should be based on solid goals that you want to accomplish—above and beyond the mere hope of changing behavior.

When you discipline, you want to teach your child appropriate behavior. In addition, your discipline can help develop the child's self-worth, avoid or resolve conflict, and promote self-discipline. Use the following goals to monitor the way you treat your child.

Goal 1: TO DEVELOP SELF-WORTH: Children who feel good about themselves will have the confidence necessary to make wise decisions and to not be easily swayed by peer pressure or the hope of personal gain.

To reach this goal, you must not demean a child or use methods designed to diminish him and make him feel worthless. If self-worth is a major goal, you'll have no use for screaming, criticizing, threatening, sarcasm or ridicule. You won't nag or push children in such a way that they rebel. You'll avoid administering discipline when you're angry. You won't spank when your child is too young to know why or too old not to feel he has been treated like a baby. You'll be careful to make the consequences fit the misbehavior so he'll never feel unjustly punished.

Goal 2: TO AVOID OR RESOLVE CONFLICT: If this is your goal you'll make sure that the "punishment fits the crime." The child should agree that your discipline was appropriate, neither too harsh nor too lenient. You'll see the wisdom of the Biblical admonition: "Fathers, provoke not your children to anger, lest they be discouraged" (Col 3:21 NKJV).

Goal 3: TO PROMOTE SELF-DISCIPLINE: A truly disciplined child is one who will behave appropriately whether you are present or not. If this is your goal, you'll discuss with the child why her behavior was inappropriate and suggest how she might handle a similar situation next time. You'll make clear the limits for her actions and show by consistency that you mean what you say.

Using these goals, you can avoid destructive punishment while teaching your child appropriate behavior. Just ask yourself before finalizing your decision about how to discipline: Will what I'm about to do lower my child's sense of self-worth? Will it cause more conflict? Will it cause me to have to stand over my child to make sure he obeys? If you answer yes to any of the above, then you had better figure out a more effective way to handle the problem.

In addition to the above disciplinary goals, here are specific guidelines for making sure your behavior will not become abusive:

1. Never discipline in anger. When emotions reach a boiling point, the discipline of your child should wait. Take a walk around the block, attack the dirty garage, yank out the weeds, play tennis, call your spouse, or pray hard before interacting with your child. When you have brought your emotions under control, it will be much easier to think of creative ways to solve the problem—ways that will not lead to further conflict or possible abuse.

2. When hasty, uncontrolled words escape your lips or when you impulsively grab or slap your child, apologize immediately. Children are resilient and seldom hold grudges if they know their mom or dad is truly sorry and making an effort to be a better parent. Determine what caused you to fly off the handle and work on eliminating the cause.

3. Treat your child not as she deserves to be treated, but as you would like to be treated if you were in her shoes or as you think Christ would treat her.

4. Put your emphasis on preventing behavior problems rather than merely reacting to behavior problems. Take time to solve problems when they are still small and fairly easy to solve, rather than waiting until you and your child are dangerously out of control. Remember the Love Cup principle.

5. Let God's Word guide your actions. Read over and over again Psalm 37:4-8. "Delight yourself in the LORD and he will give you the desires of your heart. Commit your way to the LORD; trust in him . . . . Refrain from anger and turn from wrath; do not fret—it leads only to evil." Hold fast to the promise that God will give you the desires of your heart. Many times your impulsive, rash behavior can be tempered by the realization that God wants the best for you. Trust Him. Give your life to Him, and look forward with eager anticipation for His promise to be fulfilled.

6. Take courage. Even if your behavior in the past has at times been abusive, you can change.

Although change may take a long time, it will come. Many parents were raised in homes where anger was used constantly to control people. You may feel like you spend much of your time fighting the urge to do the same. You may at times feel helpless in the face of your own uncontrollable rage. Perhaps that rage has been vented not only in abusive words but also in impulsive slaps or undeserved spankings.

You need to be aware that most people have felt like you. Few mothers and fathers have lived through the difficult years of child rearing without occasionally losing control. And people who have family tendencies toward quick anger must deal with this issue almost daily. In recognizing that most parents have trouble with anger, you are not excusing yourself. But you are allowing yourself to be human. Guilt won't help an angry person. It just adds to the pressures that tend to make human pressure cookers blow up. So don't lay a guilt trip on yourself. Just as children are resilient and forgive, so does God. And you must also forgive yourself.

If anger and losing control are frequent issues for you, then you need ask why. For some, it is because of a bad family background. Research has shown that those who are most likely to abuse their children are people who were themselves abused when they were young.

But you also need to look at your life. Is there too much pressure on you? Can you rearrange things (commitments, responsibilities) in your life to take off some of the pressure? Are you temporarily in a very demanding situation that will end soon? Can you keep in mind that the situation is temporary and then try to take things easier and relax more? Are you upset about something deep down and haven't recognized it yet? Ask yourself if there are emotional issues you need to deal with so that you'll have more patience with your children.

Also take a look at your children. Some children, such as strong-willed, hyperactive or handicapped kids, are more difficult to raise than others. The more difficult the child, the more encouragement and support you may need from others to help you maintain a positive attitude and demeanor. Otherwise, frustration and anger may become overwhelming. Don't be afraid to reach out for help. You need time off from your children so you can come back refreshed. You need more time off the more difficult the child.

Finally, especially if you have physically injured your child, you need to find help and support. Abusive behavior is usually committed in private, while in public your behavior is exemplary. That's why your closest friends, if you try to talk about your anger problem, might not believe you and may unintentionally make the problem worse by denying it. Find someone who will listen to you and understand. Hundreds of thousands of parents, many of whom are Christian, are struggling just like you.

You may be able to find a support group of similar parents

in your vicinity. Check with your pediatrician for names of such groups. Parents Anonymous sponsors local groups around the country. They provide parents with the mutual encouragement they need to work on their problem.

I've generally found that the most satisfied and effective parents are those who have a strong support system—grandmas, uncles, cousins, and friends who are willing to help whenever needed—to give parents time off to pull themselves together.

You can begin today to treat your children with Christlike love and respect. You don't have to be a child abuser!

CHAPTER 16

TEMPERING YOUR TEMPER

I know a sure method for getting your own way: Just pound your fists on the table, stamp your feet and scream! Chances are it will work. Your children will immediately take note, and most of the time they'll jump up and scamper off in whatever direction you point to do whatever you want done.

Now if little children acted this way, pounding their fists on a table, stamping little feet and screaming, we'd call it a temper tantrum and do whatever possible to stop the uncontrolled behavior. But adults? Well, most moms and dads tend to get away with it, and for too many a show of temper becomes the only method of getting kids to obey.

Parents lose their tempers and scream at their kids because it works. Children are quick to figure out that even though Mom or Dad may ask a dozen times, they rarely do anything to make sure the kids will obey until after they get so angry that they end up screaming. The result is that kids wait until they hear the screaming before they obey. They know their parents mean business then, and they'd jolly well better do what is asked immediately or they'll get it! Because kids tend to obey after they've been screamed at, their obedience serves as a reinforcement to their parents' temper tantrums. So Mom and Dad end up pounding the table, stamping their feet, and screaming more often.

It's a vicious cycle. But it can be broken, and it must because the obedience you gain through losing your temper is

101

not as valuable as what you lose. Every time you lose your temper and your children see your uncontrolled behavior, you lose their respect.

Think about it. How much respect would you have for a policewoman if she got angry with you, pounded her fists on the hood of your car, stamped her feet and screamed, "Why are you double parked?!!"

You might remember not to double park because you know that if you do you'll get a ticket. But because she lost her temper, your respect for her would be nil. Well, when it comes to parents, none of us can afford to lose the respect of our children.

There's another reason why throwing a temper tantrum, and particularly screaming, is not a good way to get obedience. It's demeaning to the child.

How would you feel if someone who was your authority (a teacher or an employer) got angry and screamed at you? You'd probably feel like shriveling up and blowing away. Add an audience, and you'd feel verbally tarred and feathered. Now, you might quickly do what that authority wanted you to do, but you'd despise that person for embarrassing you.

Children aren't that much different from grown-ups in this respect. They don't like being belittled or demeaned, especially in front of an audience.

None of us like to admit that we might, on occasion, scream at our children. We treasure our children as special gifts of God, and we don't want to intentionally do anything that might be damaging to their self-worth. We certainly don't want anyone else to know that we occasionally lose our cool. It reminds me of the story I once heard of a little boy asking his mom, "Mommy, why is it that you always quit screaming at me when Daddy comes home?" We don't even want our husbands (or wives) to know we scream at the kids when no one else is around.

When you get so upset that you're ready to explode with a bloodcurdling yell, you might try singing instead of screaming. That's what Shelly did. Shelly was usually a very calm mother. She didn't believe in yelling at her children, and she rarely even raised her voice. But one day her children's behavior really upset her.

It happened just as she was walking past the big picture window. She glanced outside and saw her three children slinging mud balls at each other. When she saw mud covering their good school clothes her anger got the best of her. She exploded. Shelly rushed to the door and yelled, "Kids . . ." and just then she noticed the next-door neighbor planting flowers right by the fence. The neighbor knew she was a Christian. What would he think of her screaming? She quickly changed from screaming to singing. Starting on the same high note that she had screamed the word, "kids," she finished her message with a little tune . . . "Will you come into the house today? Will you come into the house today?"

The moral of the story is, if you are in danger of losing your cool and damaging your child's self-worth by screaming, start screaming in the right key so you can finish with a song.

But singing is only one way to handle the screaming problem. It would be best if you could catch yourself before you got so upset that you felt like screaming. Here are some ideas:

If your child isn't paying attention the first or second time you speak, try lowering your voice instead of raising it. Go over to your child, look him in the eyes and whisper your message. I know teachers who have had wonderful control over their students mainly by lowering their voice to a whisper if there was too much noise in the classroom. The students responded by being more quiet so they could hear.

Or you might want to go one step further and try the silent method. Just go and stand next to your child and don't say anything until he or she turns and looks at you. When you have her full attention, make your request. Sometimes just placing your hand softly against the child's back and waiting will get her attention.

If nothing else works, you could always make your request over the telephone, if you have two phones in the house and a local phone system that allows you to call yourself. Call your own number, hang up and let it ring. When your child answers, pick up your phone again and you'll have her full attention.

Once you have your child's attention, make your request clearly and firmly. Then make sure you follow up so you are certain she is doing what you want. When you do this, you'll find a significant increase in your child's compliance without any harmful side effects. And, you'll feel a whole lot better by having tempered your temper!

CHAPTER 17

MAKING YOUR FEELINGS CLEAR

Negative emotions are positive—for about the first thirty seconds. That's right. There is a reason for a negative emotion. It's a signal that all is not right. Changes need to be made. And if you are in tune with your emotions, it shouldn't take you more than about thirty seconds to realize that something is wrong.

If you fail to do something immediately to change your negative emotions, then they fester and grow. Before you know it, they can become so overwhelming that you lose control. You feel compelled to act out those negative emotions in ways that will probably hurt others and perhaps you, too.

Let's say you've had a busy day. Even though you are dead tired, you cook a superb dinner for your children. They devour the food without so much as a thank-you, and the minute the last bite of fresh strawberry pie disappears—they do, too. You are disappointed that no one even mentioned the good dinner. You start to clear the table, and the stack of dirty dishes looks overwhelming.

You begin to feel sorry for yourself. "Why can't the kids help?" You don't say anything to them because you know they are studying, but the more you think about it, the more disturbed you grow. "What's wrong with those kids, anyway?" You begin to think of all the other nights when you have had to clean up alone. "It's not fair!" you say as you grab the dishcloth and aggressively begin wiping off the table. Just then, your fourteen year old innocently asks, "Mom, how do you spell encyclopedia?" You've had it. In one breath you release all that pent-up anger as you yell, "Don't ask me how to spell encyclopedia. If you can't help me with the dishes—I'm not going to help you!"

Why did you explode? Because you didn't do anything when the first feeling of disappointment hit. Instead, you tried to ignore the feeling. But it didn't go away. It began to grow, becoming more and more ugly, until you were forced to act out your negative feelings with a full-blown temper tantrum.

How can this be prevented? With a confrontive "I feel" statement said as soon as you recognize that first negative feeling. Your "I feel" statement may sound something like this: "Kids, I feel disappointed when I've gone to so much work and no one thanks me, because I like to be appreciated!" Or, "I feel angry when I have to do the dishes all by myself, because I have a book that I need to begin to read tonight."

Now in theory your children are supposed to say, "Oh Mom, thanks so much. How could we have been so ungrateful. You're the best cook in the whole world," Or, "Sorry Mom, we had no idea you felt that way about doing the dishes by yourself. Of course we'll help!" But even if they don't respond like the textbook says, your words are valuable. By saying them, you have freed yourself from having to act out your anger. You chose to do something about those feelings before they reached the explosive level—by giving your children a confrontive "I feel" statement.

There are three components to an effective "I feel" statement:

1. "I feel" followed by the emotion.
2. "When" followed by the situation.
3. And then "because" followed by the reason for your feeling. Here are some examples:

"I feel used when you leave me alone to mow the lawn while you watch TV, because there are other things I'd rather be doing."

"I feel angry when I hear rumors that you've said things about me because I value my reputation."

"I feel fearful when you go so close to the cliff because I don't want you to get hurt."

Practice saying confrontive "I feel" statements. It's a much better way to defuse your anger than throwing temper tantrums.

But beware! Your confrontive "I feel" statement, although it may decrease your negative feelings, may cause an increase in your child's. She may feel resentful because she thinks you are critizing her. When this happens don't force your point. Remember the string strategy and retreat, or you will get even more resistance, which may only increase your anger.

Let her calmly express her feelings. Just as you can decrease your negative feelings by expressing them, so can your child. So give her permission to tell you how she feels. Say, "I can tell you didn't like what I said. Now you feel angry." Then listen. Don't interrupt with statements to justify your confrontive statement. Wait until she is talked out.

After her anger has been defused, repeat your concern. For example, "But I still feel strongly about your not picking up your clothes."

Then, if necessary, listen once more—or until you feel you are both calm enough to discuss a solution. Then you can say something like this, "Well, we have a problem here. You feel _____ and I feel _____. How are we going to resolve this conflict? Let's brainstorm and see if we can't come up with a workable solution" (see the chapter on negotiating contracts). But remember, don't try to solve a problem before the anger is resolved. It just doesn't work!

CHAPTER 18

ICEBERG PSYCHOLOGY 101

In order to be an effective disciplinarian, every parent should take a refresher course in iceberg behavior. This chapter is the course you've been looking for, Iceberg Psychology 101.

A very common mistake parents make when disciplining their children is to attack the behavior they don't like rather than taking a few minutes to determine the underlying emotion that caused the problem. To keep you from falling into this trap you must train yourself to think of an iceberg every time your child does something you don't like.

Let me just review iceberg behavior so you'll know what I'm talking about. As I understand the nature of icebergs, there is always as much or more iceberg under the surface of the water as there is above. Yet, when you look at an iceberg you're not immediately aware of the bottom part. If you attempt to change the iceberg by chipping away at the top part, the iceberg adjusts itself in the water and chances are something else will emerge.

This is very similar to children's behavior. Anytime we see something we don't like, whether it's destructive behavior, sassy or mean words, teasing or hostile actions, it's like the top of the iceberg. Our tendency as parents is to get rid of the behavior that we find offensive. We spank, we yell, or we threaten to try and change that behavior. And sometimes, we are successful. That behavior disappears. But if we haven't defused the underlying emotion that caused the behavior, then the chances are that some other behavior is likely to surface. And the second behavior may even be worse than the the one we tried to get rid of in the first place.

For example, Bill defiantly sassed his mother. She slapped him and threatened to beat him within an inch of his life if he ever did it again. That seemed to solve the problem. No more sassing. But that afternoon, Mom went into her bedroom to get dressed to go shopping. She reached into her drawer to get her panty hose. To her surprise, the legs had been cut off of every pair!

She had managed to squelch one type of misbehavior only to have another, more devious type, surface. Why? Because Mom failed to get underneath the surface of the original misbehavior and take care of the negative emotion that was causing the sassing.

One day ten-year-old Bruce came home yelling, "I hate my teacher. She's stupid." His face was etched with anger; he threw his books to the floor and once more shouted. "I hate her!"

Mom was shocked by this tirade. She stormed into the room, "Bruce," she said, "I'm ashamed of you. That is no way to talk about your teacher."

"I don't care," retorted Bruce. "She is stupid and I hate her."

"Enough! I'll not have you talking like that. You shouldn't hate anyone, and I should wash your mouth out with soap for calling someone stupid—especially a teacher. Now pick up those books you've thrown all over the floor."

By this time Bruce was livid with rage. He stormed out of the room and slammed the door.

Knowing the ways of most moms and dads and how angry children sometimes become—chances are you have experienced similar situations.

What went wrong with Mom's attempts at disciplining? Mom was only trying to solve a problem. Bruce's words "I hate my teacher" were unacceptable to her. She was trying to teach Bruce to respect adults. He needed correction. But her correction only made matters worse. Why?

Let's replay the scene with a few minor changes and see what we can learn. Ten-year-old Bruce came home yelling, "I hate my teacher. She's stupid."

Mom did not approve of Bruce's behavior. She had always taught her child to respect adults and never to call anyone stupid. But she recognized that there was something beneath the surface that was causing this. She began to search for the underlying problem. Watch what happened:

"Wow," said Mom. "You are angry."

"I'll say I am," retorted Bruce. "My teacher made a fool of me in front of all the class."

"It makes you angry to be embarrassed in front of your friends, doesn't it?"

"Yes, it does." Bruce's face began to relax as he started to pick up the books that he had thrown to the floor. "I can't understand why she picked on me. It wasn't my fault. And I tried to tell her, but she just wouldn't listen." At this point Bruce's anger began to melt. His mother came over and put an arm around him and tears began to slide down his cheeks. They sat down on the couch and Bruce unloaded the whole story.

When all had been told, explanations listened to, and emotions defused, Mom asked, "Bruce, how do you think you are going to solve your problem with your teacher?" And for the next ten minutes Mom and Bruce worked on the problem together. At the very end, Mom added, "And by the way, Bruce, it never really helps when you get angry. And calling people 'stupid' doesn't solve problems."

"Yeah, I know. I'll try to remember. And thanks for listening."

When it comes to searching for the emotion underneath the misbehavior, the key is to listen, because the only way the troublesome emotion is going to be defused is to be vented by talking about it. What you want to avoid is letting the emotion be acted out in unacceptable ways.

Start listening by acknowledging the emotion you think might be the culprit. "Oh, you feel angry." "You seem sad." "It is scary when something like that happens." Your recognition of the child's emotion says to her that it's okay to be experiencing it. And immediately she feels you are on her side. Even if you guess wrong, your child will correct you. "No, I'm not angry, I'm just disappointed." Then listen as your child expresses the emotion that she has identified.

Continue to listen and acknowledge what your child has said by shaking your head or making comments like, "yes" or "oh." Let your body language express interest as well. Sometimes just being silent is the best invitation for your child to talk.

As you listen, you'll notice something very interesting happening. That strong emotion that caused the misbehavior will begin to dissipate. Then, once that emotion has been defused, your child is ready to move on to solving his problem. At that time you can say, "It's really tough to be in a situation like this, but what do you think you might do about it?" Problem solving is seldom effective when there is too much emotion. Clear, unbiased thinking is impossible in a highly emotional atmosphere.

So the next time your child exhibits unacceptable behavior, remember the iceberg effect. It may be that the behavior you are seeing is only the tip of the iceberg.

CHAPTER 19

DIVERTING DIFFICULTIES BEFORE THEY START

You should have seen it coming. It had been a miserable day for four-year-old Ricky. He had wet the bed again, and you sighed, "Oh, Ricky, not today," because it meant you had to find a slot in your already busy schedule to wash a load of bedding.

Then Scott from next door came over so early that Ricky only ate half of his breakfast even though you protested. An hour later the boys were battling over who was going to drive the new truck over the block road Ricky had worked so hard to make. In the end the road was kicked all over the room, and Scott left yelling, "My daddy's gonna beat you up!"

At that moment you walked in and let Ricky have it. "This room is a sight! You get these blocks picked up immediately." He tried to protest, saying that Scott helped make the mess, but you wouldn't listen and told him if his room wasn't clean in thirty minutes, there would be no afternoon story time. He didn't make the deadline.

You fixed a lovely casserole for lunch. Ricky took one bite and spit it all over the table, yelling, "Yuck!" You took him down from the table and sent him to his room. He warned you that trouble was ahead when he yelled, "You'll be sorry," but the baby was crying (you should have seen it coming!) . . . and an hour later Ricky's room looked like a tornado had struck. Everything on his shelves had been thrown to the floor, his wastebasket was upset, and the fresh sheets and blankets were pulled from the bed. Yes, you should have seen it coming!

Parents could divert so many disasters if we could just anticipate difficulties. A kid can only take so much pressure before he explodes. If you can see things aren't going well, forewarn your child. "It looks like you are just about ready to haul off and hit someone. That's probably not such a good idea." Your intervention at this critical time can help him gain control of himself.

Many of the things children do that parents feel must be corrected would never happen if we were more observant and helped them rechannel their energies before misbehavior occurred. Here are some effective techniques to use when you anticipate difficulties.

1. Touch control. Many discipline problems occur because the parent is not observant enough to notice that tensions are rising or conflicts are starting. Before things explode, sometimes a gentle pat, an embrace, or simply placing a hand on your child's shoulder will serve as a reminder that you are near and will help her when she needs help. If your touch is properly timed, it may prevent your child from becoming unmanageably aggressive. Touch control is effective only if you are aware of the gathering storm clouds. It should always be gentle, warm, and reassuring.

2. "Hypodermic" affection. A friendly injection of affection may give your child a quick boost over a difficult situation. This can be done verbally by saying, "I love you," or "You look great." It can be done nonverbally with a smile, a wink, or a spontaneous hug. Children need adult reassurance that they are loved and accepted. This adult support helps them to establish their own self-control.

3. Diversion. When your child becomes frustrated and can't seem to handle the situation even with adult help, diversion to another activity may help. This is especially important when children are too young to reason with. When diverting a child's attention to another activity, it is impor-

tant to find an activity as closely related to the desired one as possible. For example, if your child starts to throw blocks, a desirable diversion might be to throw beanbags into a basket or rings onto a peg, rather than sitting down and cutting paper.

4. Point out reality. Parents are often surprised at how early it is possible to reason with a child. Even tiny two year olds can understand simple reasoning when they want to. Many children become frustrated because they want to do something, but there isn't enough time or space, or the right tools are not available. They become angry and aggressive because they do not understand these limitations. Parents should take the extra time required to explain the reality of the situation and point out what can be done within these limitations. For example, "I don't have the right stuff to make ice cream, but I do have a package of pudding we can make." When you are reasoning with a child, it is important that the explanation be short and simple.

A direct appeal for the child's cooperation is often effective with older children. They like to please and be helpful and will usually listen to this direct pointing out of reality. For example, "You need to pay attention to the story because the others want to hear it."

5. Use incentives and rewards. Promises and rewards should not be used to bribe a child (such as, "If you are good today, I'll give you a surprise"). However, it may at times be appropriate to use promises and rewards as an incentive for desirable behavior. For example, "If you pick up the puzzles, we may have time for a story before lunch." It is also acceptable to use promises and rewards as an alternative to behavior or activities which are not allowed. You might say, "We can't go to the zoo today but we can go skating." Before promising anything, you must be sure you are able to fulfill that promise. If you're uncertain about whether you can fulfill a promise, then you should be careful to make it clear to your child that there are certain conditions. For example, "We can go to the

park tomorrow if it doesn't rain."

It is better to use rewards as an incentive for good behavior than to be reprimanding a child constantly.

6. Be involved. To effectively prevent problems, you have got to be an involved parent. Kids ought to believe you have eyes in the back of your head. You don't always have to give away your sources of information. It's not bad to keep a child guessing for a while: "How did Dad know I sneaked out and went to that movie?" "How did Mom find out about that cigarette?" You should be involved enough in your child's life that you can sense when she may have done something wrong, is worried, or is hiding something.

One creative mom helped keep her boys from experimenting with alcohol and tobacco by making the policy that each of them had to kiss her good night no matter how late he got home. Mom could smell alcohol or smoke a block away!

Stay in tune with your child. When you see a potential storm brewing, be willing to step in if necessary with a little extra moral support and some creative diversion tactics. You might be able to prevent some major difficulties. Diverting diasters is so much better than having to figure out what kind of creative discipline will teach your child the lesson that misbehavior doesn't pay!

CHAPTER 20

CUSHIONING CHILDREN WITH LOVE

Did you know that the kind of parent you are—whether loving, hostile, restrictive or permissive—will to a large extent determine the characteristics your children will develop? This is the summary finding of a number of studies on types of parents: loving-restrictive, loving-permissive, hostile-restrictive and hostile-permissive parents. Chances are you'll be able to see yourself in one of these types.

Some parents are very loving. They're warm, accepting, and approachable. They enjoy having the kids close. They are eager to hug, listen, encourage, and smile. A loving parent is a very nice kind of parent to have around.

But on the opposite extreme, there are hostile parents. They are cold, rejecting, and distant. "Don't bother me. I've had it! Just leave me alone!" is often the message they give.

There are also restrictive and permissive parents. Restrictive ones are those who make a lot of decisions for their children—perhaps too many—and the children are expected to consistently obey.

Permissive parents are those who allow their children to make choices whenever possible—even when they might not be equipped to do so. What limits are set are sometimes not consistently enforced.

Now let's combine these parental characteristics and see what type of behavior children are likely to develop.

If you are a loving and restrictive parent, you will probably have children who are more submissive and compliant. They will be fairly dependent and not very friendly or creative—but neat, polite, and obedient.

If you are loving and permissive, your children will tend to be socially outgoing, independent, creative, and successfully aggressive—that means aggressive enough to get good grades in school or to get a good job.

But where parents get into trouble is when their children see them as hostile and rejecting. If children don't feel loved, but their parents are restrictive, the kids often become neurotic. They're unsure of themselves and extremely shy with peers, and they often end up with poor mental health.

On the other extreme, if parents are hostile and permissive, kids tend to be noncompliant and highly aggressive, perhaps even to the extent of becoming delinquents.

The big question is, What is the most important characteristic for parents to have when it comes to child rearing? Well, obviously, if you have to choose only one, it's to be loving!

If parents are loving, regardless of whether they are more restrictive or permissive, the kids will probably do well. It's when parents are hostile and rejecting that children develop antisocial behavior.

It seems pretty clear from these research findings that you have an effect on your child's behavior. Of course, you already knew that. But it's especially your love that makes the crucial difference! You want as much love in your relationships as possible.

But that doesn't hold true for restrictiveness and permissiveness. In the case of those characteristics, you want to try to follow an ideal developmental pattern. It begins at birth with fairly restrictive parents who gradually release control to their children as they are able to make good decisions. But anytime parents are too restrictive (making all the decisions for the child) or too permissive (not imposing appropriate limits on the child) then there may be trouble ahead.

The old wives' tale that a spoiled child was loved too much

117

is just that—an old wives' tale. Too much love doesn't spoil a child—too little discipline (teaching) does! It's impossible to give a child too much of the right kind of love. Children thrive on love that is caring, respecting, accepting, forgiving, and trusting. In fact, the more of this type of love you can give, the better. Love acts like a cushion. The thinner it is, the more parental errors will bump and bruise a child emotionally. But if love is thick, parents can make occasional mistakes and children will bounce right back. They are so convinced of their parents' love that nothing can jar them.

Take my husband, Jan, for example. He grew up in a very restrictive home. His parents knew what was best for him. They had ideals that they wanted him to reach, and when he deviated from the straight and narrow—he got it. But the amazing thing is, he doesn't remember the punishments. It was only recently when his sisters were reminiscing about their childhood that they brought up the subject of how hard their dad had been on Jan. He was surprised to learn that he got whipped almost nightly during soccer season because he was so busy playing that he would forget to come home until after bedtime. The girls remember pleading his case, but it didn't do much good. Dad was firm and believed the pain of corporal punishment would eventually make him shape up. Sometimes Jan was punished twice for his misdeeds. For example, if he misbehaved in school or didn't get his lessons done and his teacher gave him a spanking, he was sure to get a second one at home.

You would think that with all those spankings Jan would have a warped personality or would at least remember the harsh punishment. But he doesn't! I believe the reason is because Jan experienced so much love during his childhood that the negatives lost their impact. Through it all, Jan never doubted that his parents loved him. And he also knew he richly deserved the punishment he got.

All parents make mistakes. Some, like Jan's father, are so restrictive that it sometimes borders on harshness. Others

118

may have been too permissive, and children have had to learn bitter lessons by trial and error. But why do so many of these kids hold no resentment? Ask them, and I think you'll find it's because they have always felt loved.

But this fact poses a problem in today's busy society. The bottom line is, children don't feel loved unless they receive adequate positive attention. But it's impossible to show attention without spending time doing things together. Therefore, many kids today don't feel loved because their parents are too busy. Thus parents today don't have the luxury of making very many mistakes with their children. That's why there's such an emphasis on democratic government within the home, understanding children, and positive techniques of communication. You can't afford to be too restrictive or too permissive. You can't afford to take any chances that your child will get the wrong message.

Why don't you start today building that love cushion, so that when you make a mistake—as we all do—it won't destroy your child. Instead, he or she will be able to bounce back on that cushion of love and say without a doubt, "But, I know my folks still love me."

(The research cited in this chapter can be found in Martin L. Hoffman and Lois Wladis Hoffman, eds., *Review of Child Development Research*, vol.1 [New York: Russell Sage Foundation, 1964], p. 198.)

CHAPTER 21

BALANCING LOVE AND AUTHORITY

Effective discipline depends on a parent's ability to balance love and authority. It is great to have fun with your children, to laugh over silly things and to play crazy games, but children can sometimes carry these activities to extremes. At that moment, you may have to say firmly, "That is enough!" At other times, you must follow a strict admonition with a hug to show that all is forgotten.

One evening Jan told our school-age daughters twice to settle down and go to sleep. But they continued talking, joking, and laughing. Finally, he sighed and nudged me, "Okay, Kay. It's your turn."

I marched into their room in military style and commanded, "That is enough. Be quiet this minute and go to sleep." Instantly the room was still. As I turned to march out again, I stopped and asked in a different tone, "Did you girls say your prayers?"

"No," they replied.

"Then you had better say them right now!" I said firmly.

Obediently, each girl knelt down and Kari earnestly prayed, "Dear Jesus, please help my mommy not to be so strict."

The irony of the situation was too much, and all three of us burst out laughing. After prayers, we hugged and kissed and parted friends.

A good disciplinarian constantly walks a tightrope between

firmness and tenderness—between love and authority. Sometimes you may tip in one direction, but you correct the error with a little tip in the opposite direction. You are not afraid to be the authority when needed, but you are equally unafraid to show love and affection.

The balancing act works best when love and authority are blended into a total approach—when you can say kindly but firmly, "I mean what I say." Harsh, unreasonable demands have no place in the repertoire of an effective disciplinarian. But if you do act harshly on occasion, an apology and a little love help to heal a multitude of sins.

The role one parent plays with the children can significantly influence the role the other plays. For example, one parent often tends to balance the love or authority shown by the other. Especially when you're overbearing with your kids, you may be forcing your spouse to lean signficantly in the other direction and become overly permissive and nurturant.

Think back to your childhood. Does this scene sound vaguely familiar?

Dad's been away all day, hard at work. Mom's been working hard at home. She was there when the kids got home. She heard all about the little squabbles at school and the huge homework assignments. The kids had had a tough day, so she didn't push the chores. They needed a little diversion, a little time of their own. But before she knew it, Dad was walking up the drive. "Kids," she calls, "Dad's home, you better get your chores done or you'll get it."

The kids dash off to do what they were supposed to do, but it's too late. Dad walks in, takes one look around and notices the trash hasn't been emptied, the leaves haven't been raked, and the tools are still scattered all over the garage. At supper Dad lays down the law and dishes out the consequences for shirking responsibilities.

Mom tries to take the kid's side. "It's my fault. I didn't remind them and they needed some free time." But Dad is determined, and nothing will change his mind.

121

That night as Mom makes the rounds for a hug and kiss and bedtime prayers, she lingers to listen and to patch up the hard feelings the kids have because they've been bossed around and pressured into doing things they don't want to do.

Have you experienced this balancing effect? When one parent is overbearing and comes down hard, often the other parent will react just the opposite.

Is this good or bad? Both. Kids need a balance of authority and love. In that way it's good. If they primarily get authority from one, then it's good for the other to balance things out. But it would be better if both authority and love could be displayed in each of the parents. Kids need moms who can meet their needs for authority and love—and they need dads who can do the same.

It's too bad when the behavior of one parent forces the other to act just the opposite, especially when the other would rather present a more balanced approach. The result is too often resentment, hard feelings, and open conflict.

It's as if parents are on a seesaw. If they both stay close to the middle—being both strong and loving—then they tend to have a close, supportive relationship. But if one gets too far out on the edge and becomes overbearing or permissive, it forces the other parent to move in the opposite direction to keep the seesaw balanced.

I hope your seesaw is balanced. If not, maybe you and your mate better talk about what you are doing to each other and make a valiant attempt to put your act together!

PART THREE

STRATEGIES
FOR CHILD
REARING

CHAPTER 22

LETTING CHILDREN IMITATE

"Monkey see. Monkey do" is an expression parents often use when referring to their children's imitative behavior. All children tend to copy the actions and words of others—especially their parents. Even tiny infants have the uncanny ability to imitate. Just stick out your tongue at a newborn. Keep repeating this action and chances are the baby will stick out her tongue, too. Isn't that amazing?

This imitative behavior is one important way that children learn to act properly. But most of us notice imitation only when it is imitation of an inappropriate behavior.

When I was teaching nursery school, I once had a four-year-old boy who behaved very strangely whenever he got angry. I finally confronted his mother. "When Keith is angry, why does he go to the wall or the nearest large object—a table or a chair—and beat on it as if he were a boxer?"

"Oh," replied his mother beginning to laugh, "that's how his father reacts when he gets angry. Just last night he got angry while we were in the kitchen, and he turned around to the refrigerator and beat on it just like that!"

Children are like sponges. They pick up whatever they see around them—even strange patterns of behavior as a way of handling emotions! That's why parents are always on stage, so to speak, when it comes to their children. You never know when your child is going to observe you doing something and copy it.

Once you've noticed how often your "sponge" copies your negative behavior, you try hard to be good. You don't eat between meals—at least not in your child's presence. You teach a children's church class every week, say thank you and please, and are quick to help the little old lady to the car. But no matter how hard you try, it's easy to slip up. One of the most common places standards seem to slip is behind the wheel. What rules do you follow when you drive? The "golden" ones? Or are you a little like the dad in the following story?

Charles was a sensitive and kind father. But something happened to him when he got behind the wheel. He hated to waste time on the road, so sometimes his priorities got a little mixed up. One time he and his family were driving back home after a long holiday weekend. Traffic was bad, and when he was forced to slip below 55 MPH he became agitated and began to change lanes to get past some of the slower cars—all the time complaining about the other drivers on the road who were causing this mess.

During one such move, his car came within a few feet of a truck's rear bumper, and he stayed there waiting to pass. He did, and a few minutes later he noticed the same truck directly behind him. He thought nothing of it until the truck moved up to within a few inches of his bumper.

Realizing he was getting some of his own medicine, he went along with it for a while, but then he grew angry and tried an old trick of the road—tapping the brake pedal so that the brake lights come on but the car doesn't slow down much.

It worked magnificently. Frightened by his apparent braking, the driver of the truck jammed on his brakes, producing a short swerving skid. All this time, the kids in the backseat were observing and occasionally saying, "Daddy, don't!"

But the game had just begun. The truck moved up again, then went into the adjoining lane and pulled up beside Charles's car. The driver lowered the window. Charles saw the irate face of his opponent and expected a brief shouting match, but instead found himself looking down the barrel of a shotgun.

Enough was enough. Charles slowed down. The driver of the truck passed, pulled in front of Charles and then slammed on his brakes to reduce his speed—and Charles's—to less than 10 MPH. Behind them the sound of screeching brakes registered the effects of the duel.

Afterward, Charles was ashamed of himself. He felt especially bad that his children had witnessed his childish behavior. He certainly didn't want them driving like that some day. So he admitted that he'd been wrong and asked the kids to forgive him. They talked about the importance of being a good witness on the road and how driving by the Golden Rule was just as important as living by the Golden Rule. If nothing else, it would keep them all a lot safer!

Charles had not been a good example for his children. Without his apology and correction, they might have ended up imitating his behavior, assuming that was the way to do things. And imagine what behavior the truck driver's kids were learning!

It's easy to get discouraged when you see your children picking up the very things you dislike most about yourself. But take courage—they also pick up the good examples. After lamenting the bad habits my kids had picked up from me, I was encouraged one day when I found my girls picking up a good habit. They were six and eight years of age, and just learning to keep their room clean.

"Girls, make your beds and pick up your clothing before we leave," I shouted above the hustle and bustle of an early morning departure. I had thirty minutes of things to do in about half that time, so I was too rushed to supervise the cleanup operation I had requested.

Five minutes before departure time, I gave the last instruction, "Get into the car. We're leaving." They promptly obeyed as I grabbed my coat and purse from the bedroom and started down the hall. As I passed the girls' room I glanced in to make sure everything was organized for the day.

"Oh, no," I sighed. Their room was a mess. Nothing had been done. Impulsively, I started to yell, but I stopped myself. After all, it was partly my fault for not supervising them more closely—and they were already in the car. Rather than get everyone upset, why not handle the situation with a little creativity?

I put down my purse and coat, picked up their clothing, and then quickly made their beds. The room looked present-able. Then I took a large piece of paper and wrote, "Dear Kim and Kari, I made your beds because I love you. Love, Mommy." I pinned the note to the top bunk bedspread where it was sure to be seen and then got into the car without saying anything to the girls about what I had done.

When we returned home Kim and Kari went to their room. I listened for their discovery. They seemed not to notice that their room was in order, but they immediately spied the note.

"What does it say?" asked Kari. Kim went over to the note, unpinned it, and read it to Kari.

"Hey, she did clean up!" exclaimed Kari as she glanced back at the beds.

"Yeah," said Kim, "Mommy sure must love us."

I waited for them to come running out and thank me—but like the nine lepers, they never did. "Well," I thought, "that surely didn't have the effect I hoped it would," and I forgot about the situation.

About three weeks later I was again checking the girls' room. This time everything was in order. Then I noticed a note pinned onto Kari's bedspread. I bent down and read it. "Dear Kari, I made your bed because I love you. Love, Kim."

This time it was my turn to be surprised. It works! Children follow good examples as well as bad. So take heart, parents. Continue being the kind of example you know Christ would want you to be. And don't be surprised when it rubs off on your children.

CHAPTER 23

MEDIA MADNESS

Parents aren't the only people that children imitate. The folk of your living room television sets are also ready models for your kids.

I was once asked to observe the eating behavior of a three-year-old child in preschool. His teacher described his behavior as quite bizzare—messy might have been a better word for it.

I arrived just as the teacher was serving cookies for dessert. The child grabbed two cookies and immediately began stuffing these in his mouth with both hands. Cookie pieces flew in all directions. I took one look and immediately realized that this child looked just like the Cookie Monster on "Sesame Street." Later I talked with the child, and he admitted that he was the Cookie Monster.

Well, Cookie Monsters are fine if they are confined within the TV screen, but they surely don't win popularity contests with overworked preschool teachers or parents who have to pick up the mess.

I am convinced that young children do model the behavior they see on TV. We hope they model appropriate behavior, but more often parents and teachers note the inappropriate. Not just messy eating—which is relatively harmless to others—but antisocial behavior that ends up causing major problems. For example, kids can pick up hitting as a way to solve problems, foul language and name-calling as appropriate ways to express displeasure, destructive and violent behavior as acceptable means of venting anger.

There have been many studies on the influence of TV, often coming to opposite conclusions. But I highly respect the work of psychologists Albert Bandura and Richard Walters on the effect of modeling.

These researchers suggest that some types of behavior, such as those that come almost impulsively and are accompanied by strong emotion, are more easily modeled than others. In fact, aggressive behavior is perhaps the most commonly modeled of all.

Bandura and Walters report a classic study where children observed adults hitting a Bozo doll (an inflated, punching-baglike figure) in an aggressive manner. Later, when the children were put in a room with the same doll, they copied the exact manner in which they had seen the adults hitting the doll. Next, the psychologists televised adults hitting the doll. After children had viewed the videotape, they copied the adult's behavior just as the children who had seen the action live had done.

Then they decided to cartoon the sequence and see what effect this had upon children's aggression. The amazing finding was that the children modeled the aggression of the cartooned figures hitting the doll as much or more than they modeled the adults hitting the doll.

Because of findings like these I don't believe you can, with safety, plunk your young children in front of the TV and allow them to observe behavior that you wouldn't want them to pick up—because chances are they will pick it up!

TV has an influence on children. YOU must determine the type of influence you want it to have. If you're worried about the amount of TV your child is watching and the influence of those programs, maybe you need some creative solutions to your TV problem. Let me share the ways that three ingenious fathers handled their family's TV problems:

Father Number One decided that the TV had to go before

his children's value systems went. He dug up the data and presented the "terrible TV" facts at a family council. The children bought his idea. They voted to get rid of the TV! So out to the garage the TV went to gather dust and wait for a final resting place.

But before much dust had gathered, Superbowl Sunday arrived. Dad remembered the set. The kids were with their cousins and wouldn't be back for hours. Why not watch the game? Sheepishly he lugged the set back into the family room, dusted off the screen, and flipped to the game. Settling back in the Lazyboy, he anticipated a great afternoon of sports.

But what was that? Someone was coming through the back gate. It couldn't be—the boys were home? What should he do? He ran to the back door, stopped the kids and sent them on an errand to the neighbors. Then he ran to the TV and lugged it back to the garage.

By the time the boys got home again, his conscience was beginning to prick. If the TV had such an influence on him that it caused him to lie to his kids, it wasn't worth it. He put an ad in the paper the next day for a used TV set.

Father Number Two bought a TV set to enjoy the evening news and the educational programs. Before plugging it in, the family made a list of guidelines to use in selecting the programs.

The next week—the very next—Dad walked in unexpectedly and found his kids tuned in to a sexy murder mystery.

"Okay, kids," he said, "this calls for a consequence. You helped make the rules and now you have broken them. What do you think your punishment should be?"

The guilty pair looked at each other. "Get rid of the TV," they said.

Dad was shocked. It was hardly what he had expected. "For how long?" he asked, figuring he could endure a day or two without it.

"A year," piped up one.

131

"Yes, a year," agreed the other.

"A year!" exclaimed Dad. "We just got the TV!" But Dad swallowed his own desire for pleasure and put the TV away. It had been packed away for eight months the last time I talked to that dad. And it wasn't missed all that much. The lesson the kids learned wasn't missed either!

The third father? This dad was pretty perturbed by the amount of time his kids were watching the tube rather than getting proper exercise. So he rigged up an exercise bicycle to an alternator and hooked the TV up to pedal power. He said his kids could watch all the TV they cared to generate. This ingenious method quickly cut the watching time down to an hour or less per day—and the result was healthier kids!

Getting rid of the TV or going to the effort to hook it up to "pedal power" are impractical suggestions for most families. There comes a time when children must learn to control their own viewing, but I believe the lesson starts with parents' control. If you can't control your own viewing habits, how can you expect your child to exercise control? Check yourself. Are you ever embarrassed when your child comes in and catches you watching certain programs? Do you ever find yourself lying about your viewing—"Oh, I wasn't paying any attention to what was on"? Your example will probably influence your children's choices more than your words!

Determine TV viewing standards for your family, and make sure the whole family (including Mom and Dad) agrees to abide by them. When my children were small I said "no cartoons." There was just too much violence and unhealthy fantasy in the regular run-of-the-mill cartoons. It was easy to make exceptions to watch TV Christmas specials or a "Snoopy" feature, but my cartoon standard saved me from a daily battle.

Your values will determine your TV viewing standards, but be wary of the seemingly innocent programs that demean marriage or family loyalty and that promote or joke about extramarital sex, divorce, male or female or racial stereotypes, and unchristian treatment of people. Just ask your kids if they would watch a certain program if Jesus were sitting with them. Asking that question can help them make wise decisions about their own TV choices.

If your family's TV viewing begins to get out of hand, you might decide to sell the TV, put it away for a few significant years, or just creatively control the viewing. But whatever you do, I hope you'll take a good, long look at the influence TV is having on your child and on your family's life. Then I pray you'll have the courage to do what you and your family feel is best.

The violence, foul language, smoking, drugs, alcohol, suggestive gestures, and immoral acts that your kids are exposed to in movies, rock music, and videos are having an effect. It's deadening their sensitivity to wrong. And whether you like it or not, their values are being influenced by viewing and hearing these things. Imitative behavior is likely to follow.

It's easy to get sucked into allowing questionable things to be viewed or heard at home. It's happened to me. I once saw this advertisment, "Fantastic film on teenage life. At last a character to model. Young girl stands up for what she knows is right." Immediately I filed the title in my mind and determined that as soon as the film became available on video, I'd get it for the kids to see. It never entered my mind to find out more about the content. What about the language? I took the review I'd read as gospel truth.

One night a friend gave the video to Kari. I should have known something was wrong when Kari asked, "Mom, did you know this movie is rated R?" But the blinders of that positive review dulled my sensitivity, and I sat down with my kids to watch.

Then it came. Horrible, filthy, smutty words. I winced. "Oh, Mom, don't listen to the words. Besides, everybody uses them." And I know, even on the Christian campus where my children attend school, I've heard some things that have made my hair curl.

So I watched for the lessons of the story. Then I needed something to finish the project I was working on, so I ran out to my office. In the few minutes I was gone my husband came home and walked in on the kids viewing a teenage party sex scene punctuated with obscene language. When he started to shut it off, they protested, "But Mom said this is a good film and we can watch it."

Moments later, when Jan related the content to me, a united parental front put a stop to it. We simply said no. You can criticize: "We're just prudish. The film was only showing what the real world's like." You can try to argue that the beauty of God's character can't really be seen unless it's contrasted with the evil of the world. These are not new arguments. I've heard it all before.

But I know that my standards have slipped a little through the years, slowly eroded by a bombardment of media that have no sensitivity to what is pure. And if my "puritanical" mind can be so dulled that I lose some of my sensitivity to evil, what must the influence of impure media be doing to my children? That's what scares me!

Our minds are such powerful computers that nothing escapes them. Every sight, every smell, every sound is captured and stored into memory. And at the right moment, with the right stimulus, it can be recalled. Research on the function of the brain has proved that. A simple probe touching a section of the brain can bring back the strains of a melody, the aroma of flowers, a scene of abuse, or feelings of euphoria. It's all there. Memory builds on memory. Thought builds on thought. Feeling builds on feeling. All of these influence the kind of person we become. Therefore, each impure thing that is allowed to enter our brains is like a Band-Aid being applied to our sensitive nature. Pretty soon, if too many Band-Aids are applied, it cushions our sensitivity to what is pure.

If you have teenagers, you've probably heard something like the following. Perhaps you see a movie with a lot of swearwords, and you express your displeasure to your kids.

Their response to your concern about the influence of this on their behavior is to say, "It's okay. It doesn't impress us. We don't even notice it anymore." Is that what God wants for His children? If we really care about our children's sensitivity, we just can't afford too many Band-Aids.

I was waiting at the airport ticket counter when an irate passenger started swearing at the airline agent about the "blankity-blank" service he had received. I couldn't believe such language was being spoken in public. Every other word was filth. My children heard it all, and we raised our eyebrows to each other. But why didn't I speak up and say, "Sir, please be careful with your language. It's really not right that I and my children have to listen to those unnecessary and degrading words!" I didn't. I would have spoken up if the guy was polluting the air with smoke—but I allowed mind pollution without any attempt to stop it.

And it's almost the same with impure sexual acts. Sex is talked and joked about without any inhibitions. Going to bed with someone is such an everyday occurrence in our Sodom and Gomorrah world that our sensitivity is dulled. We watch it on TV, even explicit sex, without wincing. We may shield our kids from these scenes, but they know what's going on. Impure sex is the subject of jokes, comedies, soaps, and almost every other TV drama. Yet when these scenes are portrayed, even on family-hour situation comedies or in the middle of an otherwise innocent movie (such as *Kramer Vs. Kramer*), do you point out that what was seen is against God's Law? If we don't zero in on these questionable episodes, it's easy for kids to think we approve!

Then there's the violence! What is all this ungodly input doing to our children? Wait a minute. What is it doing to us, too?

A friend said her son was at a party at a pastor's home where a horror video was being shown. The pastor showed no sign of agitation as he witnessed brutal murders that came about by poking fingers through eye sockets into the brain, or even when a head was ripped from a body with blood squirting into the air. But when a short sexual scene was shown where a man started to undress his companion and fondle her, he said, "I had no idea that it would be so explicit." What about all that violence? He appeared not to have noticed! And why didn't he turn it off when his sensitivity finally was aroused?

As godly parents we must take a stand—and our lives must be exemplary. The stronger the foundation of wholesome principles you lay when your children are young, the more firm will be their stand as they grow. They may kick against those standands, question, try the forbidden and rebel. But if the foundation has been carefully built, it's there tucked away in their memory, ready to function as soon as the Holy Spirit can strip away those insensitivity Band-Aids.

But if we haven't programmed those little brains with the right spiritual standards and principles from God's pure Word of life, or if we allow too many insensitivity Band-Aids to stick, then it's all the more difficult for the Holy Spirit to convict. Our children are crippled, so to speak. They can learn to walk in the purity of Christ, but it's harder. So where do we start?

First, reevaluate your own standards and behavior. You can't have one set of values for yourself and another for your children. They are quick to pick up inconsistencies. They'll call you on your hypocrisy and you'll lose credibility. It's not worth it! Make Psalm 101:3-4 your motto, "I will not set before my eyes anything that is base. . . . I will know nothing of evil."

Second, take a firm stand—and take it early. Children are more likely to accept their parents' values when their parents have set a firm foundation. Stand up to kid pressure. If you believe purity of mind and soul is important, then don't back down just for the fleeting pleasure of an hour or two of video programming. This stand isn't going to be easy with older children who are used to a more lenient position. Be gentle, but firm. Listen to their feelings. Reason calmly with them, but don't compromise your values.

Third, explain to your children the memory capacity of the brain. God designed this marvelous "computer," and He's given us good advice about the importance of quality input. "For as he thinks in his heart, so is he" (Prov 23:7 NKJV). A more modern way to put it is "Garbage in, garbage out." Your computer-literate kids will understand exactly what that means!

Fourth, fill your mind, and your children's, with the positive. The more you allow your child's mind to be polluted with impure words and acts, the more difficult it will be to stand up for what she knows is right. Little by little she becomes insensitive to the pure and will find herself being led in that direction. So fill your mind and your child's, as Paul says, with the good: "Whatever is true, whatever is honorable, whatever is just, whatever is pure, whatever is lovely, whatever is gracious, if there is any excellence, if there is anything worthy of praise, think about these things" (Phil. 4:8). And if Paul were writing in this generation, he would probably add . . . "and view these things."

Filling your kids with positive things means you have a responsibility to provide them with good media entertainment and other acceptable leisure activites to fill the void that will be left when you remove the negative. If your kids want to see a video, check first with the rental department of your Christian bookstore.

Finally, because you can't always be there to protect your child from the impurities of this world, you must inspire your child to live above his environment—to picture himself as the water lily, growing up in an impure environment but blooming clean and sparkling above it all. It's such a beautiful object lesson. The lily's roots go down deep into the good soil, so even though it grows up surrounded by polluted water, it reaches toward the sun and does not allow that pollution to stain or mar a perfect blossom.

Let's not let our insensitivity to worldly pollution and our example make it more difficult for them to choose to live a pure life. "Blessed are the pure in heart, for they shall see God" (Mt. 5:8, NKJV).

(The research mentioned here can be found in Albert Bandura and Richard Walters, *Social Learning and Personality Development* [New York: Holt, Rinehart and Winston, 1963].)

CHAPTER 24

THE PARABLE
APPROACH

Not all forms of the media are bad. TV and movies have degenerated. But stories are still a rich source of wisdom.

The job of a disciplinarian is to teach. And what better way to instruct than through a good story? Using a story to teach appropriate behavior is sometimes more effective than giving children lectures and lists of reminders about what they should or should not do. Children tend to remember the consequences of misbehavior gleaned from the lessons of stories longer than they remember admonitions or threats. Creative disciplinarians should follow the example of Christ and become master storytellers.

As you read or listen to the news or sermons, jot down the stories that have a good moral or that teach lessons you want your child to learn. Or be creative and make up your own stories, especially when you need an illustration to fit a specific situation.

Jan made up a lot of character-building stories when the children were small, but the family favorite was the nightly saga of Little Wolfy. Wolfy always seemed to get into predicaments very similar to the Kuzma children—and he always learned a very important lesson when he disobeyed or was tempted to do something wrong. The children loved these stories. Years later we mentioned to them how their daddy made up the Wolfy stories based on their own behavior and the lessons they needed to learn. They were surprised. They had no idea that their father was doing anything more than entertaining them. Yet the lessons proved extremely helpful.

There are various types of parables you might want to use as you creatively teach your children.

The question of what to tell your children concerning the dangers of questionable entertainment and other moral issues is something that thousands of parents have struggled with.

When your children ask, "What's wrong with hard rock music or PG and R rated movies?" What do you say?

Often, after parents present all the reasons they can think of concerning the dangers of certain activities, the children are still not convinced. They argue that rock music is an art form, and since questionable movies have been viewed at home, why not the theater? Or they say, "Mom, you've never been there. How can you know?"

Rather than be caught in a trap or an endless argument, tell them a parable. The following story is one I've used many times.

Once there was a Skylark family who spent a good share of the day searching for food. One day Junior Skylark heard a little man calling, "Two worms for a Skylark feather."

"Wow," thought Junior Skylark, "that sounds like a good deal. I have plenty of feathers." So he hopped over to the little man, plucked out a feather and received two juicy worms.

The next day Junior hopped over to the same area of the garden and again heard the little man calling, "Two worms for a Skylark feather." For the second time he plucked out a feather, gave it to the little man and enjoyed delicious worms for dinner.

Junior Skylark didn't really like working hard to find his dinner like all the other Skylarks, so every day he just hopped over to the little man and traded his feathers for worms.

Mom and Dad Skylark tried to warn him that trading away his feathers was not a good habit to get into, but he just ignored their advice. He thought they were just old fuddy-duddies still living in the past.

Soon summer went by and the nights began to grow cold. It was almost time to fly south. Junior Skylark, with so few feathers, felt the chill more than the rest. He was eager to leave.

Finally, moving day came. Mom and Dad Skylark flew into the air calling for their children to follow. Everyone took off except Junior. He struggled and struggled to get airborne, but alas, he didn't have enough feathers to fly. He had traded his feathers for worms.

So what is wrong with hard rock music and certain movies? Nothing, if you plan on just living a life on earth. But if you plan on heaven, then they won't enhance your relationship with the Person who has made heaven possible. It doesn't bring you closer to Christ.

Through stories with morals you can talk to your children about what their destination is. For example, encourage them to plan ways they can move in the direction they want to go and be ready for the trip, rather than trading their feathers for the worms of this world. This parable might help your child think twice about whether or not to participate in a questionable activity.

You can also take abstract Biblical concepts and relate them to the everyday life of your child with a parable. For example, many children become discouraged when they can't be as good as they want to be and end up getting punished over and over again. But even young children can be taught that Jesus will help them make good decisions and give them the willpower to do right if they are willing to ask.

The next time your child becomes discouraged about her bad behavior, after trying so hard to be good, tell her this story:

Once upon a time there was a man who wanted to build a house. "I'll help you," said his neighbor. "I've built many houses before. I have a special material called cement for the foundation of the house. No one else has it. It is strong and durable and will last a lifetime. And I'll let you have it free if you'll just ask me. In fact, I'm willing to share it with anyone who asks."

"No," replied the man. "This is my house, and I'm going to build it my own way."

So the man began to build. He mixed dirt and water to make a sticky mud to hold the stones in the foundation together. As he mixed, his neighbor came by again.

"I'm glad you are using stones for your foundation. You have to have some good material for building, but it will be of no use unless you can hold those stones together with something very strong. I'll be happy to give you cement if you just ask."

"No," said the man. "I want to do it by myself!" So he used mud to hold the stones together.

The foundation looked nice. No one could tell that it was weak—at first, that is. But soon the mud began to dry. The windstorms came; the mud began to blow away. When the rainstorms came it began to wash away. Finally, when there was nothing to hold the stones together, they began to fall away. And then the house fell down, and all the man's hard work was for nothing.

And what is the moral of this story? Just this: Trying to be good all by yourself will never work. It's like using mud instead of cement. Paul, the great apostle, couldn't even be good by himself. He said that even though he tried, he often did the things he shouldn't and didn't do the things he should (Rom. 7:15). If Paul couldn't be good by himself, how can we?

The only way it's possible to be good is to have that special ingredient, like the cement in the story. And what is it? You can find the answer in Philippians 4:13: "I can do all things through Christ who strengthens me" (NKJV).

So encourage your children to not try to be good all by themselves. Instead, ask Jesus, who has already won the battle over evil, to help them. Moment by moment, as they walk through the day, they can be asking Jesus to fight their battles against jealousy, dishonesty, discouragement—or whatever it is that is troubling them. If they want to be good, Jesus is the essential ingredient for success.

You can use other parables to encourage children to build strong character. Many children have asked, "If Jesus is willing to do so much for us, why do we have to even try?" I like the thought that God needs our effort—our choice—but He gives the blessing—the grace to cover our mistakes and the reward of heaven.

Jan made up a parable that helped our preschool children understand how the personality and character they were developing could affect them later.

Once upon a time there were two men who were planning to go on a long journey to a land beyond a narrow, rickety bridge. One man was a selfish man and the other was unselfish.

The first man looked at all his belongings. "It would be a shame to leave all these things behind for someone else," he said. "I'll just have to take them along."

He packed all his clothing, his ice skates, his baseball bat, and his basketball. What about his TV set? He must take that—and his electric train, bicycle, skateboard, and cowboy hat. Why should he leave them for others?

The second man gave away everything, except for a little money and food for the trip.

Finally, after many days the two men reached the narrow bridge. It was even narrower than they had anticipated, and it looked very rickety!

The first man stepped up to the gatekeeper at the bridge and asked for permission to make a couple of trips across the bridge so he could carry his prized possessions into the land.

"No," was the reply. "You can only cross the bridge once— and you can take no possessions."

"But I was told that I could take in one treasure—I've

never been without my TV. Please, can I take it with me?"

"No, the only treasure you can take in is the person you are!"

"But that's no treasure," retorted the man. And he stepped aside to let the second man pass.

When the second man was asked to leave his possessions, he said he didn't have any. He gave the money that he had brought with him to a woman who wanted to buy a pet for her little boy, and he gave his food and extra clothing to a blind man who was hungry and cold.

"Very well," said the gatekeeper, "you may take the person you are across the bridge."

The man eagerly stepped across the bridge and on the other side was a sign that said, "Welcome to Heaven." It was even nicer than the stories he had heard about it. It was worth giving up everything to be able to cross the bridge. He hurried back to the bridge and called across to the other man. "Give up everything. It's worth it!"

But the foolish man just shook his head as he clung to his TV set.

"Wow," said Kim as her daddy finished the story, "he was silly not to leave everything."

"Yeah," said Kari, "I'd never be that dumb."

Eager to point out the key concept in the story, Jan questioned, "What was the only treasure that could be taken across the bridge into heaven?"

"Yourself," replied Kim.

"What kind of a treasure is that?" asked Kevin.

Think about Kevin's question. If you (or your children) were taking this journey and could only take the person you are across the bridge, what kind of treasure would you be? Is your character the type that would allow you to give all you have to the poor, if that's what Christ asked of you? The Bible text in Matthew 19:21 about giving away your possessions and storing up treasure in heaven takes on new meaning with this parable.

You can use other parables to impress your child with a meaningful concept. Jesus used simple things around him to teach lasting lessons: the barren fig tree, the good seeds growing among the weeds, the lily, the sparrow. Why not use the illustrations of everyday life to teach your children lasting lessons?

Even rotten eggs can make a great lesson. For example, one day we were visiting an eighty-year-old man who had been living alone for some time. The children were hungry, and he suggested I fix some lunch for them.

I opened the refrigerator to see what the possibilities were. Some of the items looked as if they had been there for quite some time. We finally chose the eggs for an omelet.

Each child took an egg and stood by the table waiting to crack it into the bowl. The eggs all looked the same.

Kevin cracked the first egg. "What kind of eggs are these?" he asked when he saw the white and the yolk all mixed together in a yellowish-milky substance.

"Oh, my, it's an old egg," I said as I dumped it into the sink and washed out the bowl.

Kari tried the second egg. Everything was fine. So Kim was next.

As Kim hit her egg against the bowl, it exploded and spread a greenish yellow substance over the table and a putrid smell throughout the kitchen.

The children gagged and covered their noses. Cleaning up that mess took every bit of motherly persistence I could muster. And as I cleaned, I shared with the children how much like those three eggs people are. We all look pretty much the same on the outside, but it's what's inside that counts. One egg was just the way an egg should be—good inside and out. One egg was just half bad (only a few wrong feelings, thoughts, and words), but it ruined the whole. It wasn't of much use as an egg. And one egg was rotten through and through. Everything was hidden inside until the shell was cracked, and then the putrefying stench permeated the entire room. It wasn't what an egg should be.

The parable approach has helped my children remember valuable lessons. It can also influence your children to make wise decisions and take control of their lives. As they continue to recall these character-building stories, your job as a disciplinarian may slowly fade away. Having self-disciplined kids is one of the rewards of using Christ's method of teaching.

CHAPTER 25

TECHNIQUES FOR MODIFYING BEHAVIOR

I n this part of the book I'm trying to give parents as many specific, practical ideas for training children as I can think of. Behavior modification is one of those practical methods. It may sound pretty sophisticated, but it isn't. It's really a simple way to reinforce certain behaviors you like, and get rid of the ones you don't, without punishing your child. The basic idea is to praise the positive (because when behavior is rewarded it will occur more often) and ignore the negative (because you don't want the negative to be rewarded by your attention).

This method of discipline should start at birth because it doesn't require language or the child's understanding. The baby just naturally responds to attention, and when he gets it for a certain behavior, he tends to repeat that behavior more often. When I think of the admonition to "train up a child in the way he should go" (Prov. 22:6), I immediately think of behavior modification, because of all the methods this is the one that requires the closest, most consistent, nonpunitive parental involvement with the child.

Behavior modification is also one of the most effective methods you can use for encouraging your child to make long-term behavior changes. But it's not a method that works instantly.

To discourage unacceptable behavior, especially with young children, I suggest using the behavior-modification technique of "time out." When your child misbehaves, send her to a designated room or area for a short period of time— not more than five minutes. The amount of time spent in the room is not the significant factor. The time-out area works because the child is denied your attention while she is there, and thus she is not rewarded. To use this technique effectively, let your child know that you expect her attitude and behavior to change when she comes out of the room, or she is destined to return.

This method of teaching appropriate behavior should not be considered punishment; it is merely a consequence of misbehaving. Your children will accept it without resentment if you carry it out matter-of-factly, without undue force or anger. You can successfully use the time-out technique with your child if you follow these guidelines:

1. Choose ONE behavior that you would like to modify.

2. Count the number of times this behavior occurs during a particular time period—one hour, an afternoon, an entire day. It is best if you do this for three different periods and obtain an average.

3. When your child misbehaves, calmly say, "Time out for (given reason)," and take the child to the room you have selected. Be sure to tell her how long she will have to stay, or allow her to make that decision by saying, "You may come out when you are ready to change your behavior." A general rule to follow with young children is one minute of time out for each year of age.

4. When your child emerges and acts appropriately, it is most important that you give her some time and attention.

My friend, Mary, tried this technique when she couldn't get her four-year-old son, Robert, to stop hitting his younger siblings and his playmates. He hit so often that Mary was losing her friends because their children were afraid to play with Robert. Mary didn't really want to hit Robert for hitting others, that just didn't seem quite right. The last thing Robert needed was the example of his mother hitting!

I told Mary about the technique of using a time-out period whenever a child does the thing you want to change. I explained to her that behavior that is rewarded is reinforced and strengthened. So by getting angry and spending a lot of time punishing a child when he does something wrong puts a lot of emphasis on the misbehavior. It may just have the opposite effect of what you want.

Instead, with no show of emotion, simply say, "Four minutes time out for hitting," and take the child to the designated room. Remember, this is not "punishment," so the child can play or do whatever he wants while he's in the room. The time-out room is merely a place where the child can be so he is not rewarded by your attention. After the allotted time period, allow your child to come out. Don't mention his previous wrongdoing. Then when he is involved in something you approve of, spend some time with him, give him a word of encouragement, or a hug. But the next time the same wrong act occurs, back in the time-out room he goes.

I asked Mary to count how many times per day Robert was hitting so she would know if the method was being effective. Before trying the time-out method, she counted his hitting for three days. Thirty-three times per day. No wonder it was a problem.

But as soon as she began the time-out method, each day got better until after three weeks he was down to only two or three times per day, and that was something the family could live with.

Mary was so excited about this miracle method that she decided to try it on her two-year-old daughter, Lisa, who was climbing on the kitchen counters seventeen times per day. Seventeen times per day, Mom lifted her off the counter and took her to the time-out room. But the result didn't seem to be the same. Two weeks went by without any change.

Then one day, shortly after three weeks of this approach, Lisa stopped climbing on the counters. It was just as if she said to herself, "Well, I guess if I don't want to grow up in the time-out room, I'm going to have to give up climbing on counters."

The secret to being successful with behavior modification is persistence. It's a long, slow method of changing behavior, but it's effective if you're there every time the misbehavior occurs and if you do something about it. You can't be inconsistent and expect this method to work.

So if your child has a persistent habit that needs changing, and other methods of discipline just haven't seemed to work, try a time-out period. After three weeks or so of calm, consistent discipline, that habit may just disappear forever.

Behavior modification, as a method of discipline, is based on the principle that a problem child acts the way she does, not because she was born that way, but because she has learned (you might say was taught) to behave that way through the rewards or reinforcement she was given. These rewards may have been something positive like a piece of candy or hugs and kisses, or something negative, such as a spanking. A spanking is a reward if a child wants attention and if after misbehaving she finally gets your attention and you end up spanking her. The attention given along with the spanking makes it rewarding. In the case of your child hitting another, one way of not rewarding hitting would be to ignore her behavior and give all your attention to the child who was hit.

For children, immediate rewards are the most effective. When you tell your child "Thank you for putting the blocks away" two seconds after he did it, you will be more successful in reinforcing that desirable behavior than if you wait five minutes before saying "thank you." When you are trying to teach your child appropriate behavior, it is also important not to wait until he has accomplished the whole task before praising him. For example, if you want to teach your child to pick up the blocks after he is finished with them, you should start by praising him after he puts the first block away.

Once you have taught your child a certain behavior, random rewards are the most effective in maintaining it. As your child learns what is expected of her, you can withhold praise until more and more of the task is accomplished. Finally, when she consistently puts away all the blocks, you don't need to reinforce her behavior every time. The reward, as a reinforcer, then becomes more effective if it is used randomly, sometimes praising and sometimes not. At this point, not praising is really an expression of confidence that you knew all along she would do the task. It's no longer a milestone for her, and only occasional praise and appreciation are necessary or appropriate.

There are two kinds of reinforcers, the social (a smile, a word of praise, a hug) and the nonsocial (points, raisins, stars, etc.). For most children, a social reinforcement is more important than nonsocial. These are children who have a positive relationship with adults and enjoy pleasing them and having their attention.

For a minority of children, it may be necessary to give something more tangible that they desire very highly. Something to eat, such as raisins, may be the most effective. When a child must wait until lunch to eat these reinforcers, some of their effectiveness is lost. But in most cases they will still be more meaningful than something abstract like points or stars. The unique aspect of points or stars is that they can be accumulated. When the child has a certain number, he can trade them for something he wants very much, such as a toy or a trip to the park.

When you apply this method, it is important to work on only one behavior at a time. If you try to change too many behaviors at once, the child may resent having to spend so much time in the time-out room, and the method becomes a punishment.

In order to evaluate the effectiveness of the discipline, you must know how often the undesirable behavior is happening. This can be done by counting how often it happens in a certain period of time. Then, after the reinforcement program is started, reevaluate your child's behavior periodically to see if any progress has been made.

When you decide to use this type of discipline on a specific behavior with an individual child, it is extremely important that you communicate this to all members of the family so the child can be rewarded or ignored consistently.

Giving your time and attention to a child when she is misbehaving tends to reinforce negative behavior. Because of this, there are times when the very best "disciplinary" action may be to ignore the child, at least during the time of misbehavior. Not every infringement has to be dealt with by immediate action. The following situations might be best handled by ignoring:

1. When your child is frustrated or is wearing his emotions on his sleeve, the slightest comment may bring an explosion. He will probably be deaf to your pleas, anyway. Waiting until he cools down will give him the attention he desires at a time when he is acting appropriately. At this same time, he is also better able to listen and learn.

2. Leave the child alone during a temper tantrum. Children do not really enjoy throwing them; often they do it only for the effect it has on the parent and the attention it usually brings.

3. When your child is deliberately doing something to try to annoy you or get your attention, don't fall into her trap.

4. Ignore behavior you don't like but can tolerate, such as wetting the bed, sucking on a pacifier, or whining. Often your child will outgrow it.

Ignoring your child's misbehavior may be an effective method of modifying it. But ignoring does not mean being indifferent. Although you may deliberately ignore the behavior at the time, you may, a short time later, want to talk to your child about his inappropriate action so there is no misunderstanding about your expectations. If you completely ignore obnoxious behavior, your child may view this as passive approval. You must let him know in a positive way that you do not approve of the behavior and will help him learn how to behave in an acceptable way.

Modifying behavior by rewarding the positive and ignoring the negative does work, but it takes a highly involved parent. You must be observant and willing to stop whatever you are doing at the time, to take your child to the time-out room, and to have enough determination to continue the program until your child finally gets the message and demonstrates compliance.

CHAPTER 26

DOING
THE UNEXPECTED

Centuries ago French philosopher Jean Rousseau said, "Do the opposite of what is usually done and you will almost always be correct." I call the method of discipline based on this theory, shock therapy. It is doing the unexpected. It is a disciplinary technique that is effective ONLY when used very infrequently.

The most common use of shock therapy is in its more negative forms. For example, parents often stop temper tantrums by using negative shocks, such as a spanking, a cold shower, or walking away and leaving the child. Why do so many different techniques seem to work? I'm convinced that it is not the technique itself, but the fact that the parents' reaction shocked the child. It was completely unexpected. Indeed, it was the very opposite of what the child expected. The fact that these techniques are not the parents' customary way of responding is what makes them so effective. But the problem is, the more often they are used the less effective they become.

For example, although you might effectively give a cold shower to a child once, it would soon cease to be effective if it were used for every inappropriate act. Cold showering (or tossing cold water on the head of a screaming child) and spanking are examples of more negative types of shock therapy, and just because they work does not mean that they are the best techniques to use if your final goal is to rear a child with a healthy sense of self-worth. The end (whether a method is effective in producing behavior changes) should never justify the means if a child's feelings of self-worth are damaged in the process.

But I can highly recommend positive shock techniques. Surprise your child. When she expects you to be angry, smile and willingly forgive. When she expects a spanking, take her in your lap and cuddle her instead. When she expects you to send her to her room, ask her if she could use your help in picking up the mess she made. You'll be pleasantly surprised by the effect of such unexpected parental behavior.

Jeff and his dad were having a tough time communicating. It didn't happen all at once, but gradually during the teen years Jeff's attitude toward his parents became more belligerent. Now, at 15, he didn't confide in them, argued at the drop of a hat, and generally made life miserable with his constant criticism. His folks had imposed consequences by withholding privileges, but it only seemed to make things worse.

One day Jeff's dad noticed a terrific sale on an expensive racing bike—exactly the type Jeff wanted. He was tempted to buy it. Then he argued with himself. "No, Jeff doesn't deserve a bike after the way he has treated me." But the more he thought about it, the more intrigued he became over the effect the gift of a bike might have on Jeff. It was worth the risk. He purchased the bike and took it home.

"Jeff," he called when he got home, "I need your help to unload the station wagon."

"That's all I hear," replied Jeff sarcastically. "Jeff do this; Jeff do that. You'd think I was a slave or something." Reluctantly Jeff dragged himself out to the station wagon. Dad stood by watching as Jeff started to struggle with the bike box. Suddenly the writing on the box captured Jeff's attention. "Dad, what's in here? It's not a Guerciotti is it?"

"Yes," replied Dad. "That's exactly what it is."

"Ahh, well, but Dad, why are you getting a Guerciotti?"

"I bought it for you, Son. I knew how much you've been wanting one. And I wanted to make you happy."

"But, Dad, I don't deserve it. I've been acting terrible."

"I know, Son. You don't deserve it. But I love you in spite of your behavior."

That did it. Jeff's belligerent attitude was broken. He hugged his dad and apologized for the terrible way he had been treating them. The bike was an effective surprise.

Another mother told me this story: Her seventeen-year-old son had grown distant. He kept his own schedule, spending more and more time with his peers. His folks tried to impose a curfew, but he just rebelled. One night after they had gone to bed he came home screaming, "I'm on a bad trip! Don't leave me! Let me sleep with you! Please, don't leave me!" He was frantic.

It was not until then that they realized he had been experimenting with drugs. They called for professional help and were told to watch the boy throughout the night to make sure his breathing and heart rate were stable. They made room for him in their bed and let him sleep between them. All night they rubbed his back or felt his pulse to make sure he was okay. And in the morning when the effect of the drugs had worn off, he appeared a changed boy. He couldn't believe what his folks had done for him—even sharing their bed with him—when he deserved harsh punishment.

"I never realized how much you loved me until last night," he said. "When I felt your concerned touch and realized that you were willing to watch over me, in spite of the way I have been behaving, I knew I couldn't continue to hurt you as I've been doing." Once again, it was the shock of positive treatment that turned a kid around.

Caution: Positive shock therapy works, but only if it's used sparingly. Children for the most part need consistent limits, consequences, and other forms of discipline and training to help them learn acceptable behavior. But once in a while a big, positive surprise can work wonders.

CHAPTER 27

PLAYING PROBLEMS AWAY

Getting young children to obey can be a hassle. But it doesn't have to be. If you use a little ingenuity many problems can be "played" away. Children love to play games—even simple ones like "I'll pick up the red blocks and you pick up the blue ones, and let's see who can find the most blocks!" Suddenly the clean-up task becomes a game, frowns turn to smiles, and obedience is fun! Games help to avoid confrontations and to win the child's compliance.

Playacting is a great way to motivate children to cooperate—especially young children who enjoy make-believe.

For example, when you have to get a brush through a child's tangled hair and you know you can anticipate a battle, play beauty salon. "Good morning, Ms. Adams. I'm so glad you came to my beauty shop. How would you like your hair fixed today? Let's see, I think you would look nice with your hair combed like this . . ." You'll be surprised how much more cooperative a "beauty-shop customer" is than a little girl who hates to have Mommy comb her tangled hair.

Have you ever had difficulty getting your child dressed? "Hello, Sir. I'm glad you came to my men's store. How would you like a new shirt and pants? I think we have just the thing for you. Please step into this dressing room and try on our bargain for the day."

If your child is running through the house like a fire engine at full speed, say, "Remember, Doctor, this is a hospital. The patients are trying to sleep. You will just have to be more quiet as you walk down the halls."

When you meet obstinacy head-on, don't buck it; try a role reversal. "You be the mommy and pretend that I'm your little girl. Grab my hand and take me carefully to the other side of the street." Or you might say, "This room is a mess. Pretend that you are my daddy and help me clean my room because you feel sorry that your little girl has to clean it all by herself."

Play restaurant if your child balks at eating dinner. "Here is the food you ordered. It's the specialty of the house. The cook has been busy all afternoon preparing this just for you. And what would you like to drink?" To be really effective, add candlelight and drape a towel over your arm. Eating can become much more interesting when you add a little make-believe.

Maybe your finicky eater would enjoy belonging to the One Bite Club—a special club for anyone willing to sample at least one bite of everything served. Here is how the club got started at the Bennett's house. Ruth's kids were such finicky eaters that the dinner table had become a battleground. Then Grandpa came to visit. He sat halfway through one mealtime, and that was enough. "What this family needs is a One Bite Club," he announced.

"What's a One Bite Club?" the children asked.

"It's a club where all the members eat at least one bite of every food that is served. And then, once a week, the club members have a party and go out and play miniature golf."

"When can we go?" the children shouted.

"Not until you sample each food on the table."

"Yuck," they turned up their noses.

"Now wait," said Grandpa. "It's not that bad. All you have to taste is one spoonful—and it doesn't have to be a big one."

"This much?" asked one, as he held up a half-filled spoon of broccoli.

"Oh, no," said Grandpa. "That's way too much."

Now it was the children's turn to be surprised. The child

shook off a little, and with his spoon one-fourth filled, he asked again if this was enough to join the club.

But once again Grandpa said, "Too much."

Finally, there was such a tiny amount on the spoon that the child eagerly put it in his mouth and announced, "I couldn't even taste it."

"Then," said Grandpa nonchalantly, "you might want to take a little more." And without force the child helped himself to a second, and bigger spoonful. That night they celebrated.

You might want to make up some One Bite Club membership cards for your family. Research supports the idea of a One Bite Club. Parents who encourage their children to eat at least one bite of a new food have children with a wider range of food likes than those parents who either force their children to eat everything or don't care what they eat. The One Bite Club is just another game to encourage rather than force compliance.

The One Bite Club might solve the problem of tasting new foods, but what if you want your child to finish his plate? Play the game of guessing how many bites are left. Let each member of the family guess a number, and then the child has to eat everything so you'll know who is the winner. The fun of this game is that the child can decide how much food he puts into each bite, controlling the results!

A written message can often be more effective in averting problems than personal involvement. Kari and Kevin were out watering the garden one afternoon, and Kari had the hose. I overheard an argument and a threat about a water fight, so I quickly penned a note. "Dear Kari, please do not water Kevin. He is not a flower. Love, Mommy (from Africa)." I put the note in an envelope and sent it special delivery with Kim. By the time Kari put down the hose and read the note, tempers had cooled and Kevin had escaped to the safety of the house.

Because obedience is such an important lesson for children

to learn, we should use every bit of creativity that the Lord has given us to make it easy for children to obey. We want obedience to become a habit. And behavior only becomes habitual if it is repeated often. So, instead of forcing children to obey and making the lesson distasteful, why not playact problems away and make the obedience lesson not only effective, but fun, too.

You can use fun to break habits. Do you have a little Linus walking around your house with a pacifier in his mouth and a threadbare, nondescript rag trailing around behind? Most children have a difficult time giving up these comfort devices. When Mom or Dad decides the security crutch has to go, the result is too often a tug-of-war.

But there is another way if you're a game-playing parent. You must first realize that there's nothing wrong when infants and young children have pacifiers, security blankets, and special toys. So don't rush a reluctant child into prematurely giving these up. But when you feel it's time for your child to move on to more grown-up behavior, you might want to try the habit-breaking game Raylene played with Shawnee.

Shawnee was 2 1/2 years old and still very dependent on her special satiny blanket. She also needed her pacifier to go to sleep. Raylene didn't have a problem with the blanket, but the pacifier was beginning to be a nuisance, and she suspected that it should be no longer necessary.

Dreading the inevitable trauma this transition would cause, she kept putting it off until one day she ran into a friend who also had a little girl about Shawnee's age. And they had a new puppy with them! After appropriate admirations were expressed, little Beth announced, "I traded my bottle for the puppy."

"What's this?" Raylene asked. Her interest sparked.

"Oh," said Beth's mother, "Beth was so attached to her bottle that any attempt to take it away was met with tears and pleading to have it back. Since she had her heart set on getting a puppy, we got the idea that she could get the puppy by trading her bottle for it. And you know, it worked! Since she now has something she very much wanted, and since it was her own decision, I didn't come off looking like the big, bad mommy. And she has no reason to beg and plead for her bottle anymore."

"What a marvelous idea," Raylene exclaimed. "I'm going to try it with Shawnee's pacifier."

Shawnee wanted a doll carriage, so Raylene suggested that Shawnee trade her pacifier for one. Shawnee thought about the possibility for a couple of days and finally decided it was worth it. At last the time came for the transaction. After the doll carriage was purchased, a very solemn 2 1/2 year old handed the clerk her precious pacifier, and with shining eyes proudly placed her baby doll into the carriage and wheeled it out of the store.

So, if you find yourself wishing your little Linus would give up his bottle, blanket, or pacifier, why not wait until he wants something badly enough to be willing to trade for it. If it worked with Beth and Shawnee, chances are it will work for your little Linus, too.

You can also use games to help out at bath time. I've received a number of letters from parents telling about the fun things they have done to get their kids to take a bath. Some of these are so clever, I think they're worth sharing.

First, try coloring the bathwater, and chances are your child will want to hop in. Just add several drops of food coloring to the water. If it's made be put into our bodies, it certainly won't hurt the outside. And it won't stain the bathtub or your child's skin. Chances are she will watch wide-eyed as the color swirls and is gradually diluted with the water. The father who gave me this idea used red food coloring and told the story of Moses in Egypt when the sea turned red like blood. His child was fascinated. You could also use two colors at once and make bath time a lesson about primary and secondary colors. But limit the colors to two unless you like the look of muddy water.

Another idea is to finger paint on the walls of the shower—just don't use regular finger paint! Instead, put a lot of Ivory soap flakes in a little warm water and whip it up with an electric beater until it's like whipped cream. You can add a little food coloring if you want. Be sure to have a rubber mat on the shower floor so your child won't slip. Then when he's finished, just turn on the shower or take a big sponge and wash everything off. The shower and the child will both be cleaned in the process.

Bathtub time is always more fun when you have some bath toys to play with, but many moms and dads complain of having bath toys all over the tub or bathroom floor. If this is a problem in your home, give your child a fishnet and challenge him to capture all the floating toys before the water drains away. Then the toys can be kept in the fishnet to drip-dry in the tub. You can either leave them in the tub until next bath time, or put the toy-filled net away under the sink or in a closet.

Why not turn that bathtub into a lake of sailboats? It won't cost a thing, because kids can make these boats all by themselves. Just take half of a walnut shell, chew a little bubble gum, stick it inside and put a toothpick into the gum for the mast. Then cut out little squares of cloth for the sails, and you can have a fleet of boats in no time. Actually, anything that floats can make a boat: jar lids placed upside down, pieces of wood, paper cups.

One dad combined bathtub time with storytelling time. The kids loved hearing all the stories about when he was a boy—and even Bible stories took on new meaning the way Dad told them.

Finally, one parent suggested that you gather some objects from the house and ask your child to sort them into those things that float and those that sink. Bath time can be an important learning time and with a little creativity, it may become a highlight in your child's life.

But in some families it's bedtime, not bath time, that's a

big problem. If you've found bedtime is bedlam time, maybe it's time for a game.

I'll never forget the mother who told me she had tried everything and still her kids were resisting the idea of getting on their pajamas and getting into bed. Suddenly, inspiration hit! "Hurry," she called, "I've got a prize for the first kid in bed wearing someone else's pajamas!" You should have seen those kids trade pajamas—like their lives depended on it—and before you knew it, they were in bed. Then, of course, everyone looked so funny dressed in PJs that didn't fit that Mom made them get back out of bed while she took a picture.

If you have young children who don't seem to respond to your request to go to bed, you might get more compliance if you offer them an animal ride to bed. During the preschool years our kids were carried to bed on monkeys, giraffes, ostriches and even sharks. They loved it.

My friend, Elmar, came up with an innovative bedtime game to solve a problem he was having with his son, Chad. During the first three years of Chad's life, Elmar was a super-busy medical student and resident. Time was not his own; he practically lived at the hospital while his wife, Darilee, took the major responsibility for caring for the kids.

With those years of training over and a practice established, Elmar decided he wanted to spend more time with his son. He especially wanted to be the one to put Chad to bed, read him a story, say prayers together, and tuck him in with a hug and kiss.

But Chad would have nothing to do with this. When well-meaning Dad tried, Chad cried for his mommy. So Darilee came and tucked Chad into bed. Elmar decided he wasn't going to take no for an answer. He devised the following strategy. When Darilee started to tuck Chad into bed, Elmar quietly crept into the bedroom on his hands and knees. Because of the way the crib was situated, Chad could not see anyone entering the room. Then Elmar picked up a small rubber ball and tossed it over the end of the bed where it landed beside the surprised little boy.

Chad, of course, was surprised. But he did what any normal three year old would do; he picked it up and tossed it back outside the crib. Elmar caught it and tossed it again. Chad was intrigued with the game. Back and forth the ball went, accompanied by Chad's squeals of delight. Finally, Daddy popped into sight, hugged and kissed Chad, whispered a good-night prayer, and tucked him into bed.

The next evening Chad said to his mother, "Mommy, I want Daddy to put me to bed just like he did last night." So Mom put Chad into bed while Elmar crept in quietly and tossed a soft toy into the crib. Back and forth it went, until Elmar popped up and hugged and kissed his son. This became the bedtime ritual.

A couple of weeks later the family was entertaining a guest. Just about bedtime the guest asked Chad if his dad ever read stories to him at bedtime. "No," said Chad with a gleam in his eye. "He just throws things at me!"

If a happy bedtime means throwing things when other parents are reading bedtime stories, why not? With a little creativity you can both be winners.

One of the main goals of creative discipline is that of encouraging self-discipline, and I've found that games have been extremely effective. For example, when Kevin was younger, he rarely left for school with a clean face until we stopped giving commands and started playing a game: "Whoever walks outside the house with a dirty face gets to empty the wastebaskets." (Of course, that is a game of imposed consequences. But we acted as though we were playing a game rather than disciplining.) Soon I was having a hard time finding anyone to empty the trash—but faces were clean. Nine thousand, three hundred forty-two reminders did not get through to Kevin, but one simple game made the difference.

When you initiate a game to teach your child responsibility, it's important that the rules apply to the entire family.

Our family uses an electric toothbrush, and for years, Jan and Kevin were constantly reminding me to take my toothbrush off the appliance when I was finished. Kevin finally decided that the family should play this game: "Whoever forgets to take his toothbrush off has to go to his bedroom and count to twenty-five." Wouldn't you know, Kevin was the first one who had to count to twenty-five! But the game also helped me to remember this simple task.

If you decide to try this technique, make sure that every family member agrees to play and has a say in setting the rules. Games lose their value if they cease to be fun or if the consequences of losing are not consistently carried out.

If you're trying to teach your children to be thorough when doing a task you might want to try variations of the next two games.

Why not hide pennies under various items where the child needs to dust? If you don't expect the item to be picked up and dusted under, then leave the penny partially visible. Tell the child how many you've hidden and see if he can find them all.

One mom paid her child a quarter for sweeping the leaves off the patio, but asked for a penny back for every leaf that was left when he was finished. She didn't get anything back!

Playing make-believe can also be an effective way to help children discipline themselves. Sue was the mom of two preschoolers who seemed to pick up every dirty word, unkind behavior, or moody characteristic they ever observed. And there were some neighborhood kids that exhibited a lot of what was to her unacceptable behavior. What should she do? Keep her children home all day, away from bad influences?

She tried keeping them home, and her children were miserable. They wanted to play with friends. After a couple of days at home, they felt like prisoners—and she like a jail keeper. That was no way to live. So, she changed her attack.

First, she focused on making their backyard into a children's paradise. She ordered a truckload of sand for a giant sand pile and purchased water hoses, buckets, shovels, plastic trucks and other sand toys. Before she knew it, word had spread through the neighborhood.

But whenever a child came to play or was caught sneaking over the back fence, Sue would say "You may play here. But I'm the King of this domain, and you have to obey my rules or you will get kicked out and can't come back for two days." Then she very carefully showed them the boundary of her kingdom—where the fence line was—and explained the rules.

Rule number one: No bad words. No swearing or taking God's name in vain. She gave them examples of words that she had heard the neighborhood kids say that were unacceptable, so they knew without a shadow of a doubt what was expected.

The second law in her land was the golden rule: "Treat others as you want others to treat you."

Sue made herself a crown to wear to remind the children that they were guests in her kingdom. And the result was unbelievable. Kids whom she had heard previously arguing and calling each other names were playing side by side in perfect harmony.

One time the bully of the neighborhood tested the rules. He got mad, threw sand and shouted obscenities at a friend who accidently stepped on the road he was building.

Sue plopped on her crown and gently, but firmly, escorted the offending child off their property. She explained very carefully that he was banished for two days. She then called his mother so she'd know why he'd been sent home. After that, no one challenged the rules.

Why do games like these motivate self-discipline? Games take the work out of doing what you have to do. Children set on being stubbornly resistant suddenly become captivated by the challenge of the game. Before they know it they are having a good time obeying. Since kids love to play games, what a great incentive they are to be self-disciplined enough to be able to participate.

I once read that if parents would play more with their children, their children would love and respect them more— more than if they were always serious and acted their age. This is true because kids love playful people. Children establish close ties with people whom they sense enjoy being with them. And if they have this relationship with their folks and other authority figures, they won't resent an occasional correction when it needs to be made.

I didn't have any trouble playing with my preschoolers. I wore the skin off my knees creeping around the floor playing piggyback, and I found every secret hiding place in our yard playing hide-and-seek. I've enjoyed pitching balls to Kevin, although I don't do it as often as he wishes I would. Young children love to play with their parents, but teens enjoy playful parents, too.

I was intrigued by the story Gloria Gaither tells about her playful mother. She had a slumber party one night and when it got fairly late her mother called up to them, "All right girls. It's time to go to sleep."

The firmness of her voice meant business, so they turned off the light and crawled into bed. They were trying their best to get to sleep when they felt water sprinkling on their faces. They finally figured out it was coming in through the bedroom window. They ran to the window to investigate, and there was Mom in her robe and slippers with the water hose.

That was too much! The girls raced downstairs to get back at her. As they ran through the kitchen, they were surprised to find a huge pan of popcorn waiting for them. Then they all sat down to enjoy the midnight snack while Mom told them ghost stories in the dark. Gloria fondly remembers the night when her mom forgot to act her age.

Moms and dads can be a lot of fun. But too often we get caught up in everything we need to do, and we forget to laugh. It's been so long since we have been kids, we have forgotten how to act silly, play jokes, and be a child among our children. And I'm speaking for myself.

One day my daughter said to me, "Mom, I wish you were more like Sherry's mother. She's so much fun to be with. We can tell her anything, and she just laughs with us like another teenager. She never lectures us—even though I know she'd correct us if we needed it."

Well, I want to be fun, too. And I can, if I just determine not to take life so seriously. Occasionally I need to step off my parental pedestal and forget about all my weighty adult responsibilities. I need to take a deep breath, let down my hair, put on my grubbies, and play with my kids.

After all, King Solomon says, "Everything is appropriate in its own time. . . . So I conclude that, first, there is nothing better for a man than to be happy and to enjoy himself as long as he can; and second, that he should eat and drink and enjoy the fruits of his labors, for these are gifts from God" (Eccles. 3:11-13, Living Bible). Aren't your children the most precious gifts of all? Why not play problems away if at all possible? When you do, you'll find yourself enjoying your child and your job as a creative disciplinarian twice as much.

CHAPTER 28

GRAB A
CAMERA AND LAUGH

What do you do when your child innocently creates such a monumental mess that all the king's horses and all the king's men couldn't put it back together again? Life with children can sometimes be frustrating. But instead of getting upset, throwing a temper tantrum or going AWOL, I have a suggestion: Laugh! The ability to laugh in an unbelievably bad situation is a safeguard for a parent's mental health.

Just in case your child hasn't yet tested your sense of humor to the limits, let me tell you about a laughable moment a mother shared with me. It was three-year-old Jason's bath time, so to entice him into the tub Mom put a couple of perfumed bath-oil balls into the water. Soon the balls dissolved. Jason wanted more. Thinking the balls looked like cherry tomatoes, he headed to the refrigerator, found the basket of tomatoes and dumped them into the water. Then he climbed back into the tub, waiting for them to dissolve. Nothing happened. Back to the refrigerator. What about eggs? Or pickles? Would they dissolve? Why not try.

During all this, Mother was on the phone. She knew she shouldn't leave Jason unattended while in the bath, but the phone had rung and she rushed to answer it. When she didn't come back, Jason tried some more experimenting. Would lettuce float? What about cabbage, cucumbers, peppers, parsley and carrots? He emptied the vegetable bin into the bathtub. Then he began pouring in milk, leftover soup, tomato sauce and cottage cheese. Sitting in the middle of a milky pink sea of vegetables and eggs was certainly more exciting than his ordinary bathtub routine.

Just as Jason was beginning to crack the eggs, his wonderful, loving and usually sane mother walked into the bathroom. You can imagine what happened. She flipped! She began to laugh and cry at the same time. Throwing up her hands and shaking her head, she backed out of the room shouting to her husband, "That's it! I'm leaving this house and never coming back." She promptly walked out the front door and headed down the street, still shaking her head in disbelief.

Jason, quite puzzled and shocked by his mother's drastic reaction to such a "small" matter, took his mother's words literally. He jumped out of the tub, grabbed a towel in one hand, and raced down the street after her shouting, "Mommy, Mommy, please come back home!"

That was a few years ago. Jason is now a healthy six year old who has learned the difference between perfumed bath-oil balls and cherry tomatoes.

And mother? She has survived, too. What did she get out of the gigantic mess? Well, she learned there is more than one reason for not leaving a child unattended in the tub. Plus she has an absolutely marvelous story that is sure to bring gales of laughter when a party gets dull.

The next time your little one innocently coats the bathroom with cold cream, or pulls the 400 sheets of tissue from the box one by one, or pours the goldfish into the toilet, or empties your bureau drawers and dumps your clothing and a full box of laundry soap into the washer, or pours a couple of gallons of water into the 40 lb. bag of dry dog food . . . don't panic.

First, take a couple of deep breaths and pray for patience. Next, run for the camera (because nobody but another parent is likely to believe your story). And then LAUGH!

Of course, it's easier to say than do. About a month after I heard this story and used it for a radio script, the unbelievable happened in the Kuzma house. We had just gotten a new carpet in our family room, hallway, and bedrooms. It was a beautiful light beige, and everyone agreed that we should take off our shoes when we came in from outside to prevent the carpet from getting soiled.

Kim, who was fifteen at the time, was especially proud of the carpet and took upon herself the responsibility of reminding the family to remove their shoes.

One afternoon we went out visiting, and Kim accidently stepped on some tar. Kim had no idea the bottoms of her shoes were covered with it, and without thinking she walked across the new carpet with her shoes on, leaving black globs of tar with each step.

When she finally reached her bed and looked back over the rug, she couldn't believe what she'd done. In stocking feet she came running out of her room, calling to me to grab my camera.

"Why?" I asked.

"Because I've just done the unbelievable!" I looked down at those 29 tar spots on my beautiful new carpet and was just about to scream. My face began to cloud with a look of horror when Kim added, "Mom, laugh. You're supposed to laugh." Well, we all had a good laugh finally and began the clean-up job.

Then, just a few weeks later, the unbelievable happened again. This time it was Kevin and his cousin Troy who were the culprits. They wanted to play basketball, but I'd parked the car in the driveway. There would be plenty of room if they could just push the car down the driveway about ten feet. They pushed and pushed, but the car wouldn't budge. Then they remembered that the emergency brake was on, so one of the boys opened the car door and released the brake, then they both began pushing.

But without the brake, the car started backing down the

drive with increasing speed, heading straight toward the neighbor's grapefruit grove. There was no time to stop it. How it missed hitting our walnut tree and the irrigation standpipe, I'll never know. The car finally came to a stop as it hit the soft branches of the grapefruit trees—unharmed!

The boys were just calling for Kim to drive the car out of its unusual parking place when I walked out on the scene. They gasped when they saw me, and then Kevin yelled, "Mom, grab a camera!" Of course we all knew the context of that statement and laughed. I think the boys learned a lifetime lesson from that incident. But without the bathtub vegetable soup story, I probably would have wrung their necks—or at least given them a verbal lashing.

I hope you'll remember the bathtub vegetable soup story the next time your child innocently does the unbelievable. And then for your child's sake, why don't you pray for patience, grab a camera—and laugh!

CHAPTER 29

MAKING A GAME OF BEING AN ADULT

Today's various non-Christian psychologies are generally based on a view of human beings which is not wholly accurate. Most of them do not take into account the spiritual side of humanity. Others, like behaviorism, treat people like physical machines. But despite these weaknesses, we can learn things about people from these theories. Behavior modification, for example, can be an invaluable tool in discipline. There is some truth in most of these psychologies, and all truth belongs to God.

Transactional analysis (T-A) is one of these modern psychological approaches. It is a theory which talks about why people react in certain ways. T-A can help you and your children analyze why they react the way they do when pushed instead of led. This is the theory behind T-A: Each person has three styles of personality within them.

1. The PARENT personality is one of superiority. This is when a person feels he knows best and lets other people know. It's opinionated, bossy, degrading and unwilling to listen to other viewpoints. It makes others feel inferior. You speak from your PARENT personality when you say, "That's no way to do it." "Watch out." "You never were very good at that." "You should think before doing."

2. The CHILD personality is one of inferiority. It's an immature personality—emotional, impulsive, and irresponsible. This personality is exhibited when a person jumps to

conclusions, acts on emotions, rebels, belittles herself, or fails to make decisions. The CHILD personality in you might say such things as, "I hate it when you do that." "Don't tell me what to do." "It wasn't my fault." "I always make mistakes." "I don't know how to do it." "You're always right." The CHILD personality is the way youngsters (or grown-ups) usually act when they feel pushed.

3. The ADULT personality is the mature, thinking personality that treats others as equals. When you operate in this personality it makes people feel good about themselves, and the result is that they usually treat you in the same respectful way. If you could just learn to always interact with your children using your ADULT personality, you would probably experience very little conflict. But the problem is that your PARENT or your CHILD too often dominates your interaction.

The PARENT personality in you almost always causes the CHILD personality to respond, no matter what the age of the person. For example: "Put those shoes away right now" (your PARENT) usually causes the child to respond in his CHILD personality, "Don't tell me what to do," or "I don't know how."

In contrast your CHILD personality almost always causes the PARENT personality of the other to respond. For example: "I've had it with you kids!" (your CHILD) might get a response like, "Mom, that's no way to behave," or "It's your fault what happened," which would be your child's PARENT personality speaking.

Once you explain T-A to your children they can have a better understanding of why they may be getting treated the way they are and can begin accepting some of the responsibility for the conflicts they have been having with Mom or Dad.

Travis, a very wise father, used T-A to try to prevent further conflicts his son, Justin, was having with his mom. Mom was on the war path. Justin had promised to have his room picked up by breakfast time and to feed the animals and

174

finish his homework before 8:00 each evening without any reminders. In return, Mom had promised to let Justin decide on his own bedtime.

But Justin thought that at 14 years of age, he should be able to set his own bedtime regardless of what he did during the day. Each night the battle over bedtime grew more intense. Finally Mom declared to Dad that she had had it, and she was giving Justin a checklist of duties that he had to do or there were going to be severe penalties. Dad knew that Justin and his mother had been on such lousy terms that the checklist at this time would infuriate Justin. So trying to divert a catastrophic battle, Travis went into his son's bedroom just after he had gone to bed, sat down next to him and began to talk. Travis reviewed T-A with Justin.

"Now if a person is behaving in his CHILD personality by being irresponsible and spouting off impulsive statements, how is the other person likely to respond?"

"In their PARENT," Justin responded correctly.

"And how does the PARENT act?"

"Bossy and superior—like they know it all," said Justin.

"And how is a person likely to respond to this bossy PARENT?"

"In his CHILD personality, by saying whatever pops into his head and being childish."

"And if you don't want someone to respond in his PARENT, what do you need to do to get him to act in his ADULT?"

"React in your ADULT." Justin knew T-A theory well.

"Okay Justin, let me explain what's about to happen tomorrow morning. You have been acting like a CHILD all week, not carrying your part of the bargain to clean your room, feed the dogs and get your homework done. So your mother has been acting as a PARENT treating you like a CHILD, forcing you to go to bed at the time she has decided. And the result? You've been acting like a CHILD and rebelling.

"Your mother, now, is so angry that she has decided to give you a checklist with a severe penalty attached, which is a typical PARENT response.

"But chances are you're not going to like that. You now have the choice of acting like a CHILD and making your mother act even more like a PARENT. Or you can surprise her and act like an ADULT and bring her back to her ADULT so she will be kind and understanding to you. It's up to you."

"What do you think I ought to do to get her into her ADULT?" asked Justin.

"Well, if I were you, I'd get up first thing in the morning, clean my room and offer to help her with breakfast. That would be acting in your ADULT—in a very responsible way. Then I'd bring up the subject and say something like, 'Mom, I've been thinking that I've been very irresponsible this last week, and I'd like to apologize.' And I have a feeling if you continue to act in your ADULT that your mom may even forget about making you a checklist. But if she doesn't and you still get a checklist, say, 'Thanks, Mom, this will make it a lot easier for me to remember what I should be doing.' And if you continue to act in your ADULT, I don't think you'll have any more trouble."

The next morning a very responsible Justin approached his mom in a very ADULT way, and the crisis was averted. Once children get the idea that they have this kind of power over their parents—that they can change bossy parents into civil ones—then acting responsible isn't work, it's a game of behaving so you can keep Mom and Dad acting like ADULTS!

It's really fun when you begin using your understanding of T-A to monitor your own actions and words so you don't evoke the CHILD or the PARENT in others. Remember, you've got to act in your ADULT if you want your child to respond in her ADULT!

Once the whole family gets into T-A, you can begin analyzing why each of you are acting the way you are, and without criticizing say, "Oops, your PARENT is showing!" or "Careful, I think I may have heard your CHILD responding." It becomes a game. Your kids will love "correcting" you. When you become aware of how your behavior effects others, you'll be more careful to stay in your ADULT, so your child will be more apt to respond in her ADULT! Remember, your ADULT personality doesn't get angry and threaten or push and punish. ADULT personalities are masters at leading others in the way they should go, and the result is a lot more compliance. Why don't you play a little T-A with your family today?

CHAPTER 30

NEGOTIATING CONTRACTS

C hildren, obey your parents." That may be a Biblical admonition, but the older your children, the more they would like to be included in the decisions that affect them.

I vowed to honor and obey when I said "I do" and married Jan, but I would still be resentful if I felt Jan were pushing me by demanding, "Pick up the laundry, mail this package, and invite these people over for Saturday night." I'd much rather hear him say, "Honey, I'm very busy today, but I think I can be home for dinner on time if you can pick up the laundry, mail this package, and invite the guests for Saturday night. Would that be possible?" I'd much rather be asked than told.

Children feel the same way. If you involve them in decisions that concern them, they will be much more willing to comply with your requests. That's why moms and dads need to become masters in the art of negotiation. Negotiation overcomes negative resistance because it involves both parties in determining the solution to a problem. It allows for compromise and creative solutions. Plus, negotiation often results in a contract so both parties know exactly what is expected of the other. That limits the hurt feelings when the consequence clause must be imposed.

In order for negotiation to be effective, a child must be (1) verbal enough to discuss possible solutions; (2) smart enough to understand what she is contracting for; and (3) mature enough to keep the bargain that she has made. How does negotiation work? Follow these steps:

STEP 1: Define the problem with your child. For example, John has not been brushing his teeth regularly, and he rebels at every reminder. So you approach him about his behavior. "John, I have to pay the dentist's bills and when you don't brush your teeth, the bills can increase. What can we do together to make sure that this important job gets done?"

STEP 2: Brainstorm together about possible solutions to the problem. Working together you might come up with the following list: put a reminder note on the table; do not serve dessert anymore until John begins to brush regularly; buy an electric toothbrush; get better tasting toothpaste; have a special code as a reminder; give John a nickel every time he brushes and have him return a nickel if he forgets.

STEP 3: Decide together which possibility is most acceptable. John thinks that he would remember if he had an electric toothbrush. If he forgets, John promises that he won't get angry if he is reminded with the code words, "Billy Goat." When he hears the code, he will brush his teeth immediately. A consequence clause should be included at this point. If he resists after being reminded, he must forgo dessert at the next meal.

STEP 4: Decide when the contract will be put into effect.

STEP 5: Indicate in some manner that you both agree on the contract. Write it down, sign it, shake hands, or seal it with a kiss.

STEP 6: Evaluate the effectiveness of the contract periodically. If the contract is not working, go back to the bargaining table and draw up a new contract.

Negotiating a contract involves a child in the decision-making process. It is excellent training for a child's inner control system—a necessity for self-discipline. The following guidelines will help you use this method most effectively.

1. Don't approach a problem by placing blame solely on your child. This will only antagonize her and prevent a successful resolution. Instead of blaming, put the emphasis on

how something effects you. Start your message with the pronoun "I." For example, "I get upset and angry when I hear so much quarreling." This is much less offensive to a child than an accusing "you" message, such as "You kids quit quarreling right now. All you do is fight with each other."

2. Be willing to bargain. Don't come to the bargaining table with a rigid solution in mind. Be flexible.

3. Be supportive—not antagonistic. Show your child by your behavior and attitude that you are the ally, not the enemy.

Negotiation can be used for determining appropriate consequences. Decide ahead of time, through negotiation, what should be the consequence for a certain misbehavior. For example, no supper until the dog has been fed, no TV until the homework is done, or if you don't help with the meal preparation, you must do the dishes. If the child agrees on these consequences, then when he goofs up, all you have to say is, "What did we decide should be the consequence for this?" The child can't (or shouldn't) argue with the fairness of this type of punishment once he has agreed to it.

Caution: You must be sure your child agrees to the contract because he feels that the consequence is fair—not just because she fears your anger and rejection. You never win if your child gives resentful compliance. This only leads to hostility and later rebellion. As a parent, you don't just want compliance from your child, you want willing compliance. Otherwise, you'll find yourself pushing your child to obey and getting resistance.

The White family is a good example of how negotiating contracts can creatively solve your discipline problems. The White's family policy had always been that the children should earn the money they need for school activities and other items above and beyond the basic necessities. They did this by taking on jobs around the house. Mom kept a list of jobs with the amount of money she was willing to give for each one.

The system worked well until Linda's sophomore year in high school when she decided she was too grown-up to help around the house. She had more important things to do than earn extra money for spending. But at the same time her "want" list doubled, and she soon depleted her savings. That's when Linda began taking advantage of her parents. Band tour was coming up. She needed $75. Then there was a varsity jacket, a new dress and shoes for the banquet. When Mom restated the family policy that she should be earning this extra money, Linda willingly agreed. But she needed the money now. What was she supposed to do?

Mom bailed her out the first couple of times and loaned her the money. But Linda, even though she had plenty of opportunity to do odd jobs around the house to earn the money back, took no responsibility for her debt. Mom decided that she'd give no more loans. But Linda desperately needed the money. They had come to an impass. It was time to head to the negotiation table to see how the problem could be solved. The result was the following loan agreement that would encourage the children to earn their necessary spending money before they needed it.

LOAN AGREEMENT

I agree that whenever I borrow money I will pay a 10% loan origination fee.

I understand that I will be allowed 2 days for every $5 loaned to pay the loan back in full and that for every day late a 10% late fee will be charged.

I also understand that no further credit will be extended until each loan is repaid.

Signed: _____
_____

Date: _____

The family also decided that it would be important to work

out a plan so the children could begin early to earn the money they knew they would be needing for future activities. For example, Linda's brother wanted to attend three weeks of summer camp which would cost $100 each week for a total of $300. This is the contract they worked up for him.

CONTRACT TO EARN MONEY FOR SUMMER CAMP

I will earn the sum of $100 per camp for a total of $300. I will earn the total amount per camp before I attend. If I do not earn the necessary amount, I will forfeit the camp.

If I have earned the total of $300 two weeks before summer camp is to begin, then I understand Mom and Dad will give me $25 for spending money.

Signed: _____

Date: _____

At the same negotiation session, Mom came up with another contract that would allow the children another way to earn money. She really wanted to encourage her children to read their Bibles. This was so important to her that she said she would be willing to give them $1 for every chapter read. Then she made up tally sheets for them to record the chapter read and the date completed. The children loved the new challenge and eagerly dusted off their Bibles!

The older your children are, the more you will enjoy negotiating contracts as a way of solving problems. Master the technique early so you'll be able to get as much use out of it as possible. Start today by writing down an offensive or irresponsible behavior that your child might be willing to change with an attractive contract. Don't delay. Head to the bargaining table.

CHAPTER 31

PARENTING PRODIGAL CHILDREN

Thousands of conscientious Christian parents suffer excruciating pain over the prodigal behavior of their children. The kids grow up in the church, they learn all the right verses, Mom and Dad have had family worship every day, yet the children defiantly turn their backs and choose worldly pleasures like drugs, alcohol, and sex.

How do you parent such a prodigal child? Do you kick him out—or welcome him home? The answer isn't clear-cut. What the child needs (more than ever before) is unconditional love along with limits. Kids must feel accepted, but if they choose to hurt others with their rebelliousness, then there must be consequences. In love, you cannot allow your child to mistreat anyone—including yourself.

The prescription of unconditional love and limits is easy enough to verbalize—but the difficulty comes in the application. First, let's talk about limits. Rhonda was a prodigal living at home. Heavy metal, cultism, alcohol, and pot were a common part of her life-style, and it clashed head-on with the values of the rest of the family.

With three younger and very impressionable children, Mom felt she must take a stand. As much as she loved Rhonda, she could not allow her to flaunt her deviant lifestyle and destroy one or all of her vulnerable siblings. So, with tough love Mom laid down the law. Her daughter could do as she pleased elsewhere, but her activities were not to

183

disturb the rest of the family. She gave Rhonda three rules for conduct in the house:

1. No signs of drinking or smoking in any part of the house. For example, no beer cans in the refrigerator or ashtrays by the TV, and no smoke smell in the rest of the house.

2. You can listen to whatever music you want to in the privacy of your own room as long as it can't be heard outside your room.

3. You may not entertain friends in your room with alcohol, smoking, cultish activities or heavy metal.

Rhonda's mother told her that as long as she was willing to abide by the established family policies, she would be welcome to stay. But if she chose not to abide by them she must leave. Rhonda's mother said, "I pray that you will not have to leave, but if you do I will help you find an apartment, pay two months' rent to help you get established, and then you'll be on your own. If things get tough, I want you to know I will not help support the life-style you have chosen."

"If you want to come back home, you'll always be welcome, but the same conditions apply. If you break them the second time, it will be entirely up to you to establish yourself elsewhere. Only once will I pay the rent to help you get established.

"I believe I am doing this for your own good. I love you and always will, but I cannot allow you to destroy the lives of those around you. I pray that someday in the future you will understand."

That next week, Rhonda defiantly threw a pot party in her room. Mom calmly walked in, asked the kids to leave, and when they hesitated she told them the consequences. Since pot was illegal she would have to call the police. That was the end of the party—and the next week Rhonda was in her own apartment.

I can't report that Rhonda immediately repented with a complete change of life-style. Like most prodigals—even the Biblical one—it took awhile. But not shielding Rhonda from the consequences of her behavior was an important step in the recovery process.

One of the means that rebellious children use to manipulate their parents is blame. They blame their folks for the mistakes the kids have made. And they keep their folks bending over backward, making excuses for their kids' behavior. If your kids blame you for the mistakes they make, it's time you stop playing their game.

Bernice was overcome with guilt. Her teenage son was having a hard time, and it was all his mother's fault. At least that's what he kept saying. When she tried to help him out, she would get, "Mom, just butt out—you're always messin' things up for me." And when she left him alone to solve his own problems, she would get hit with, "You don't even care about me—if you did you'd get me out of this mess!" No matter what she did, she was always wrong—and she began to feel guilty about not being able to do anything right in her son's eyes.

You've heard of child abuse? Well, I believe this constant blaming of parents for kid's mistakes is parent abuse. Parents have to stand up for their own rights.

That's what Bernice did. She said, "Enough. You may not treat me like this. You make your own choices and are responsible for your own behavior—regardless of the way you were treated in childhood or what I do today. You determine your own destiny. Sure, I made some mistakes in rearing you, but I did my best. I just didn't have all the answers and in my frustration and ignorance I mistreated you occasionally.

"But I ask you to forgive me for my mistakes. I can't go back and do it over. Saying, 'I'm sorry,' is the best I can do. And, by doing this, I hit the ball back into your court. You can now choose whether to forgive me or keep blaming me and allow your resentment to cloud your life.

"No longer will I play your blaming game and feel guilty when you accuse me of causing your problems. In fact, I want you to know that if you continue to play this game I will walk away, hang up, or ignore whatever you are throwing my way. I love you with all my heart and I want what is best for you. I don't want your life eaten away by bitterness and resentment. But, there's nothing I can do to prevent that if you choose to keep dwelling upon your bad memories of childhood and your preceived injustices of the present."

The result of this speech was a very surprised boy. He took the medicine in silence. Then after his mom was finished, he looked her straight in the eye and commented, "That was some speech!" But you could tell the way he said it that even though he may not have liked it, his respect for his mom went up a notch or two.

If you at times feel your children are abusively blaming you for their mistakes, why don't you remember Bernice's speech, stand up tall, take a deep breath, and let your kids have it. Stop playing the blame game. That's the only way you'll win. And it's the only fair way to set them free to become responsible persons.

Finally, when you find yourself the parent of a prodigal child you must be filled with unconditional love. Limits and love cannot be separated. When parenting the prodigal your affection must not be dependent on your child's behavior. You must act respectfully toward him or her even when you can't approve of what he or she is doing. This type of love has an uncanny drawing power. The story of Russ is a typical example of this.

As a young man, Russ went to Viet Nam and got mixed up with all kinds of things, including drugs, sex, and tobacco. His parents were obviously disappointed when he came home a chain-smoker. Russ knew how offensive smoking was to his dad, and the first time he stepped into the home with a cigarette in his hand he expected to be kicked out. Instead, his dad put an arm around him and said, "Russ, you know how I dislike smoking, but if that's the only way I can have you home, I guess I'll just have to get used to it. You're more important to me than the smoking."

186

Russ was so shocked with his dad's response that that was the last time he ever smoked in Dad's presence. He just respected his dad too much to offend him.

Of course, that is just one example—and for every positive one, there are probably a dozen negative ones. But regardless of the statistics, the winning principle remains the same: Love heals alienation while guilt and bitterness only make it fester.

So, think about it. Just how accepting are you? Could you treat your prodigal with respect even if she didn't deserve it? Could you open your arms to your wayward son and lovingly introduce him to your most respected friends or would you be ashamed to admit his existence?

Sharon and her husband hadn't heard from their son in months. David had run away—only telling them he was going to Los Angeles. They asked him to write. He didn't, but that didn't keep his mom from hoping and searching. Finally, through an old friend, Sharon was able to get an address of someone who might know his whereabouts. She wrote expressing love and a longing to see him. Would it be possible for him to meet them at the Los Angeles airport? She and Dad and Grandma and Grandpa would all be there. They were directing a tour to the Holy Land and would be taking off at 3 p.m.

It was just a shot in the dark. Would he get the message? And even if he did, would he make the effort to get to the airport when he hadn't even bothered to call collect for almost a year? Sharon's faith was weak.

This was a highly esteemed Christian family. Sharon's father was a pioneer in Christian radio. His programs had aired for over fifty years on hundreds of stations across the world. He was a giant among the Christian leadership of the country. When he led tours to the Holy Land, it was an honor to be included.

Finally the departure day came. The entire tour group was assembled in the boarding area. Sharon and her husband, along with Grandpa and Grandma, were surrounded by important members of the Christian community. Sharon wondered if her son had gotten the message. But it was such a remote possibility, she pushed it from her mind. With the excitement of the trip, she had almost forgotten her letter.

Just minutes before they were to board the plane, she noticed a shabby-looking couple break through the crowd. The fellow's hair and beard were unkempt and uncut. His baggy shirt (unbuttoned to the navel), cut-offs, sandals and beads clearly identified him as part of another culture. There was so little to the girl's dress that it left no room for imagination.

Sharon's immediate thought was, "How could anyone go out in public looking like that . . . and the nerve of them to push their way through the middle of the tour group." She was just about to turn away when she recognized her son and ran to him with arms outstretched and genuine tears of happiness. "Oh, David. You came. You came!"

Then, without any hesitation or show of embarrassment, she turned to the crowd that was watching and announced, "I would like to have you meet our son, David." There were more hugs and kisses as Dad and grandparents greeted David and welcomed his friend.

That moment was the beginning of David's homecoming. He didn't just rush home, burn his clothes and don a three-piece suit. He continued to search for himself, traveling the world and even delving into some Eastern religions. But he did begin writing, and two years later David sent his belongings home. He wasn't far behind.

Our prodigal children haven't treated us any differently from the way we have, at times, treated our Heavenly Father. Aren't you thankful our Father is going to greet all His prodigal sons and daughters with open arms? Shouldn't we do the same for ours?

CHAPTER 32

YOU CAN'T
WIN THEM ALL—
BUT GOD CAN

You may try all the disciplinary techniques in this book and still your child might have problems or exhibit some objectionable character traits. Don't be discouraged. Give God a chance to work in your child's life.

When Sara was about six years of age, she developed an irrational fear that the house would burn down. Often at night she would complain to her mother, "I can't go to sleep. I'm afraid of a fire." Her voice would quiver, she'd cry and cling desperately to her mother, "Don't leave me. I'm afraid." Her mother tried everything she could think of, talking about the fear, reasoning with her, and explaining how the smoke alarm would warn them, but nothing seemed to help.

Finally late one night as her mom was kneeling down beside Sara's bed talking to her about this fear, her mom said, "Sara, we haven't been able to solve this problem, so let's ask God to take away your fear." Mom put her hands on Sara's tummy and began to pray. She asked Jesus to make the spirit of fear leave Sara, to give her peace and to help her trust in God. Sara went to sleep peacefully that night and never again experienced that intense fear.

Peter had a habit of throwing temper tantrums when he was with his father. He would scream hysterically and then hold his breath until he actually passed out. Peter's mother tried every new technique she learned about on Peter but the tantrums continued without a change. Finally she mentioned the tantrums to a Christian counselor.

The counselor suggested that they first give the problem to the Lord. As they prayed together they were impressed that Peter was experiencing rejection. In discussing this possibility Peter's father confessed that he had rejected Peter at the time of his birth, favoring instead his twin brother. The father repented of his negative feelings toward his son. They then prayed that God would heal the damage done to Peter's sensitive spirit. Peter never again held his breath to the point of passing out.

Jerry was accident prone. Throughout his growing years he had broken dozens of bones and suffered numerous cuts and sprains. His mother had become fearful of having him leave her sight. She was especially concerned about his going away to college. She shared her concern with her women's Bible study group, and they began praying for her fear and for Jerry's safety.

As she prayed she remembered that during her pregnancy she had experienced a terrible fall and was terrified that she had harmed the baby. This anxiety over Jerry's safety had continued during his growing years and seemed to increase with each accident. Once she released her irrational fear to God, she sent Jerry off to college in perfect peace. Four years later she related the story to him. "That's interesting," Jerry commented. "I haven't had an accident since I came to college."

Teresa suffered night terrors. Screaming hysterically in her sleep, she described the horrible experiences she was dreaming about, but the next morning she remembered nothing. Sometimes these terrors lasted so long that it kept Mom or Dad awake much of the night. After a long time they decided to pray for Teresa's deliverence from these irrational night terrors. They went into Teresa's bedroom shortly after she was asleep, placed their hands on Teresa's head, and asked God to do what they had not been able to do. They continued praying like this nightly as the terrors decreased in frequency.

After a few weeks Teresa was sleeping calmly through the night.

Kyle had a terrible battle with his father before bedtime one night. He shouted "I hate you" to his daddy who had slammed the door of his bedroom and threatened him if he were to get out of bed again. He fell asleep with rebellion in his heart. This had happened once before and for days afterward Kyle had exhibited the spirit of rebellion.

Mom silently prayed for wisdom to know how to handle this situation without demeaning her husband and causing further conflict. She waited until both of them were asleep, then tiptoed back into Kyle's bedroom and prayed over her peacefully sleeping son. She asked that God would remove the spirit of rebellion from his heart and restore within him a loving respect for his father's authority. The next morning Kyle woke up as if nothing had happened and was once again a sweet, compliant child.

I'm telling you these stories to bolster your faith. God does answer prayer. The answer may not come as quickly as we feel it should. God's timetable is not the same as ours. And God's answer may not be what we expected. But when we trust Him we can rest in the assurance that His way is best.

Working with God on behalf of our children is a cooperative effort. We have a part to do—that's why I wrote this book and why I'm so thankful you have read this far! We must be responsible disciplinarians. But we must also give our children to the Lord and ask Him to constantly be working on their behalf.

If you would like to tap into God's wonderful power, I'd suggest you start by praying a blessing on your child's personality like the Bible patriarchs so often did. Ron tried praying a blessing on his children's personalities and wrote me about his experience.

Dear Dr. Kay,
    I'd just like to share with you an idea that came

to me while reading Genesis. I became impressed as I read over and over again about the Patriarchs blessing their children according to their knowledge of that child's personality and the future. Why not bless my children according to their personalities?

First of all, I had to become convinced that each child's personality was a gift of God—its strengths and its weaknesses. I became aware that a child's strengths if not properly channeled would become his weaknesses. A strength of personality turned toward one's self will destroy; turned toward God will bless and minister.

So the direction of my blessing was to ask God to enhance the strength of my children's personalities and turn those traits toward Him. I did not want the children to change in response to Daddy's wishes; I wanted God to do the changing in them. So each night after they were asleep I would enter their room, stand over them and pray a blessing.

My oldest daughter is ten. Her most obvious personality trait is high sensitivity. She was very sensitive to herself. Her feelings were easily hurt. Tears were free flowing. "That's not fair" was a key saying, but spoken only when she felt something was not fair to her. I prayed a blessing for her that she would be sensitive to God and others. Within two weeks change was apparent.

Previously when disciplined, all she was concerned with was the punishment. "Am I going to get a spanking?" "How many swats?" "How long of a restriction?" Now the response is, "I have done wrong; I'm sorry," and tears of genuine repentance. She has become sensitive to the feelings of others and their hurts. She is developing into a person with the ability to comfort others.

I could tell of other responses in my other children but time is too short. . . . Ron closed the letter saying that it was his hope that other parents would pray a blessing on their children's personalities and experience God's wonderful power.

Perhaps we, as parents, try too hard to change our children's God-given personalities when we should be channeling their personalities into God's ministry. God made our children the way they are for a special calling He has for them. I believe they can be strong-willed for Jesus, hyperactive for Jesus, talkative for Jesus—or sensitive for Jesus!

But it starts with trusting in God, who gave them their personalities, that He can turn their personalities toward Himself and use them. We must pray for this, otherwise Satan will use those same personalities to cause conflict and heartache that will ultimately destroy our children's happiness and hope for the future.

Our children are not our own—they are a gift from God. If we feel we own our kids, then it's easy to treat them as we feel like treating them, and sometimes those feelings aren't too good! If we think we own our kids then we tend to make most of their decisions and we carry the responsibility for their behavior. Then when they choose to become independent, we feel a devastating sense of loss.

If at their 18th birthday they're pretty good kids, then we feel an inflated sense of pride. We did it! But if they've rebelled and made some pretty lousy choices then we suffer tremendous guilt.

I think a much more healthy view of child rearing is that our children are a gift to us from God. He retains ownership and ultimate responsibilty for them throughout their lives. We, then, are responsible to God for the way we treat His children. We shouldn't abuse them in any way or treat them as we feel like treating them. Instead, we should treat them as God Himself would treat them. And the only way we'll know how God would treat His children who are growing up in our homes is to keep the channels of communication open between us and their Owner.

Sure we'll make mistakes, but He promises to fill in where we fail. It's amazing! God gives us His children even though He knows we're not perfect. But He expects us to do the best we can and to keep learning how to improve our parenting skills so we can continue to meet the needs of His children at each stage of their development.

Because God has created our children with the power of choice, He knows that some will go astray. But if we have done our best and asked forgiveness for our mistakes, that's all God asks of us. He doesn't want us burdened down with guilt. He has ways and means of reaching those children, if we will just release them to Him and trust Him.

If you view your children as a gift from God, then when they become independent you won't feel a bitter sense of loss. You'll feel that sense of honor for being chosen to perform this important work of using your creative talents in raising a child for God. I hope today, you feel greatly honored!

WHAT ABOUT SPANKING?

I know you're wondering why the discussion on spanking is in the appendix. Well, this is a book on creative techniques of discipline, and I couldn't with good conscience include it in the main body of the book. Yet I knew that when you finished reading this book, your first question would be, "And what about spanking?" So, here's my philosophy: Too many parents, without thinking, spank their children because they believe that a spanking is synonymous with doing the will of the Lord.

Here's an example. The car in front of us was Christian. You could tell by the bumper stickers, "God Loves You," and "Honk, if you love Jesus." On the back window was a rainbow with the words, "Praise the Lord."

Inside the car were two young mothers. One was driving and the other was switching. Every few minutes the mom in the passenger seat would turn around to the two preschoolers in the back and switch first one and then the other with a two-foot switch off a tree.

If only I could have tuned in on the conversation to detect the reason for such behavior, then perhaps I could be more understanding. The children couldn't have been doing too much wrong, strapped in their seats as they were. But whatever it was, that mom was sure giving it to them.

My children couldn't believe what was happening. "What is that lady doing?"

"She's praising the Lord and punishing the kids," I replied tongue in cheek. My children were indignant. "But that's not how you praise the Lord!"

"Unfortunately," I explained, "there are a lot of parents who read Proverbs 22:15, which says, 'The rod of correction shall drive foolishness far from him' (NKJV), and figure that if beating a child is good—then the more the better!"

But actually the opposite is true. The more spankings a child receives the less effective they become. Take my brother, for example. He was always getting a licking, and it didn't change his behavior. In fact, I remember one day he came home and asked Mom to spank him because he broke a neighbor's window. She complied, and a few minutes later he left the house with a clear conscience. He had paid his debt to society. A spanking for him was an easy way out of whatever difficulty he managed to get himself into.

For other children, spankings only increase their defiance. One of the saddest stories I have ever heard was of the little boy who refused to point to his belly button after his parents had asked him to. They were encouraged by their friends to spank the child into submission because the "Bible says so." The child either didn't know where his belly button was, or he stubbornly refused to play such a foolish game, and they ended up beating him to death. You must realize that some children have become so defiant because of the forceful treatment they have received that they will endure tremendous pain rather than obey. Once you begin physically punishing a child there is a very thin line between a hard spanking and abuse.

It's especially difficult for me to understand how some people can advocate spanking babies, even newborns, to teach them that they can't have their own way. Spanking babies is abusive.

Most of the time if babies misbehave it is because they get frustrated, or they just plain don't know any better. Prevention is the best answer. If you can just meet the needs of the baby before she gets frustrated and out of control, you won't have problems. And if you do, spanking isn't the answer.

Sally was only eight months old when she threw her first temper tantrum. Mom could tell Sally was out of control. Why else would she be screaming, kicking, and banging her head? Well, if Sally couldn't control herself, her mom would have to supply the control Sally needed. So she picked Sally up and calmly, but firmly, held her close until Sally grew tired and relaxed in her arms.

It would have been meaningless to slap Sally, because she was too young to understand why her mother was causing her pain. Spanking a tiny baby for this type of behavior only makes things worse.

Daryl was almost one when he discovered the newspaper and started to rip it up. Dad said no in a firm voice, shook his head, and took the newspaper away. When Daryl started to cry Dad diverted Daryl's attention and then gave Daryl extra attention when he began playing with something appropriate. After a couple of weeks Daryl would reach for the paper, hesitate, and shake his head. Daryl was learning that his dad meant what he said. Daryl was learning to choose to be obedient. This type of discipline—or teaching—needs to start at a very early age.

But, you ask, why not spank him? Won't he learn a lot faster that way? Why fool around with methods that take more time? Why? Because children, like rats, will try to avoid pain. Therefore, it's true they often will not repeat a behavior that brought them pain. And occasionally, it may be necessary to teach an important, instant lesson of safety by slapping a little hand reaching out for the hot burner, for example. It's a lot better to do that than to doctor burned hands.

But young children catch the wrong message when their parents inflict pain and they are too young to know why. Spanking a child for wiggling on the changing table is an example. Babies naturally wiggle. But at such an early age it is impossible for them to perceive, "Oh, I was hit because I

197

shouldn't wiggle." All they know is that the person with whom they are most familiar also causes them pain. Growing up with this type of treatment often makes the child feel bad about himself and causes mistrust.

Jesus wants babies to grow up feeling good about themselves. Especially during that first year learning to trust Mom and Dad is important. If there is a chance pain might get in the way of your baby learning these important lessons, why take that chance? Let's make sure we give our babies Christlike discipline.

Spanking is a negative shock technique. It can be effective. But the more frequently a spanking is used, the less effective it becomes. In fact, I'm convinced that the only parents who use spanking successfully are those who don't spank their child for minor infractions. Therefore, the spanking surprises the child and shocks her out of her negative behavior and rebellious attitude.

I confess I've spanked all of my kids, but I'm not proud of that fact. I don't think spanking is necessary for effective parenting. I do believe that when a spanking is used there is probably another more creative method of discipline that would have been just as effective. But if you are at your wit's end, and nothing creative seems to pop into your head, and you feel the urge to spank, please PRAY and then consider carefully these guidelines.

1. Only spank your child when he is willfully defying your authority, and milder measures have failed. Avoid this method when your child has acted inappropriately because he is too young or immature to know better. Don't automatically spank a child for challenging a request you have made. Willful defiance is not the only reason for disobedience. Do not overuse this method.

2. Never spank your child when you are angry. It is too easy to spank too hard or too long. There is a very fine line between a hard spanking and child abuse.

3. Tell your child beforehand whether the spanking is a

one-strike, two-strike, or three-strike spanking. There should never be more than three strikes.

4. Spank immediately after the misdeed. If you wait too long to administer a spanking, it won't be effective.

5. Make sure your child clearly understands the reason for the spanking. A child should be able to feel that her punishment "fits the crime." If she can understand the reason for this disciplinary action, you won't have to contend with feelings of resentment or injustice.

6. Spank your child in private. It is demeaning and embarrassing to the child to be disciplined in front of an audience.

7. Your child should experience enough discomfort to change his rebellious attitude. If, after the spanking, he slams doors, calls you names, or stares you in the eye and says defiantly "That didn't hurt," the spanking was ineffective. Calmly repeat the spanking once or use a more effective disciplinary technique immediately.

8. Plan a love experience after the spanking. If your child is young, take her in your lap and rock her. If she's older, go to her in five or ten minutes. If she is not yet ready to talk, return in another five minutes. Talk about pleasant things. Offering your time and tenderness after such an experience will convince her of your love.

9. Consider your child's age. In order for this technique to be effective your child must be old enough to realize that this isn't your usual method of disciplining. He must be able to reason from cause to effect to see the justice of this type of discipline. An older child's self-worth can be shattered by a spanking. It can be a demeaning experience. I would caution you to avoid spanking before your child is two and after he is eight or nine.

10. Finally, the rapport you have with your child will determine whether or not you can safely use spanking as a method of shock therapy. Diana Baumrind, a psychologist, has found that spanking produces passivity, timidity, and fearful conformity when it is used impulsively by repressive,

restrictive parents. But when parents are warm, responsive, flexible and have a good rapport with their children, an occasional spanking as fair discipline is linked to self-reliant, independent, and confident behavior. (Reported in *Today's Child*, November 1978.)

Should you spank or shouldn't you? That's a question I can't answer for you. You'll have to decide what's best for your child. But if you make an occasional mistake, don't be overwhelmed with guilt. Children are resilient when they know they are loved, and they are quick to forgive when they know you're trying to do your very best to be the kind of parent God wants you to be. Reassure yourself with this jingle:

> The definition of perfect parenting is easy to express, Just err and err and err again, but less and less and less.

I AM SPECIAL Books

. . . develop your children's awareness that
God made them unique.
. . . increase your children's confidence
and self-esteem.
. . . help your children understand God's
love and care.

My Own Special Body
I Can Talk to God
When I Am Sick
Me, Myself, and I
My Family Is Special
My Friends Are Special
Oh, Yes! Oh, No!
Good for Me!

Chariot Books

CHRISTINE HARDER TANGVALD has worked
with primary and preschool children for over twenty
years. She is also the author of the My Friend Leif
series for ages 3-5, available from Chariot Books.
JUNE GOLDSBOROUGH has illustrated many
picture books and educational materials
for children. She works from her home
in Southern Illinois.

Ages 1-3

Do you want your child to read well?

Whether it's reading a cookbook or the Bible, whether it's reading a textbook or an exciting novel, the ability to read with ease and understanding is a foundation for life. We want our children to be good readers, because many important benefits in life come to those who can read well and who like to read.

But no matter how well your children read, the good news is that you can help them become even better readers. *How To Raise a Reader* will show you how.

How To Raise a Reader

- How to prepare a child for reading even before he or she begins school
- How to make a book lover out of almost any child.
- How to choose books for children-- recommendations of the best read-aloud books for infants to ten year olds, including the best Christian books for kids.
- How to help improve your school's reading program.

Author Elaine McEwan knows what it is to help kids read. Besides being the mother of two readers, she has been an elementary school teacher, a librarian, and is currently principal of an elementary school in West Chicago, Illinois. Elaine is a graduate of Wheaton College and holds a doctorate in education from Northern Illinois University. And she loves to read.

David C. Cook Publishing Co.
ISBN 1-55513-211-1   52118